Text and illustrations by Abria Mattina.
Cover images by:
Kate Rose | Origins Digital Curio, Creative Market
Freepik | kjpargeter

Maps for Fantasy Creatives

50 Inspiring Templates to Sketch and Plan your Locations

created by
Abria Mattina

Contents

Contents

Contents

Contents

WELCOME TO YOUR BOOK OF FANTASY MAP TEMPLATES

Whether you're a writer, an artist, a gamer, or a role-player, I hope you find this book of map templates inspiring and useful.

The Fantasy Maps for Creatives book contains fifty map templates and legends. The legends include lists to record cities and towns, landmarks (e.g. mountains, rivers, etc.), bodies of water, and provinces and districts. Keep track of your own markings, such as roadways, with the Lines & Symbols space. You'll also find blank pages for notes, rough drafts, or anything else about your creations you wish to record.

Map pages are made with plain lines, which make it easy to interpret the landforms and bodies of water any way you wish. The scale of these maps is entirely up to you — map a single city or an entire continent. Coastlines and other natural borders are rendered in varying amounts of detail, for those who want minute topography and those who just want the broad strokes.

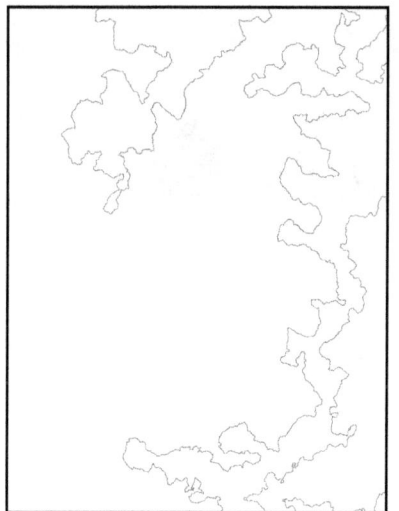 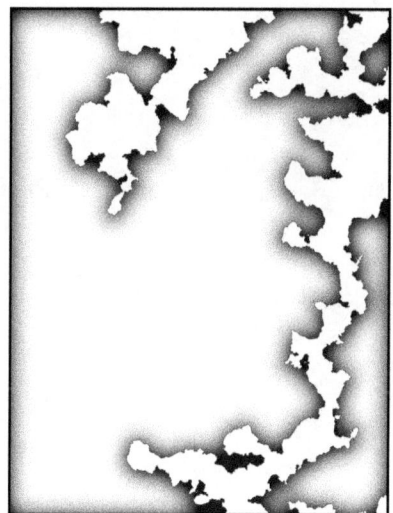 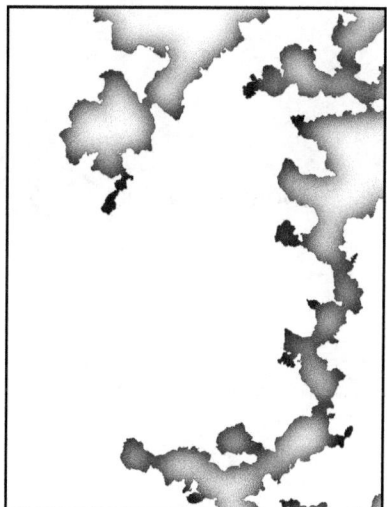

Share your creations on Twitter or Instagram, @AbriaMattina.

MAP

Story:

Cities

Landmarks

Bodies of Water

Provinces/Districts

Lines and Symbols

Scale

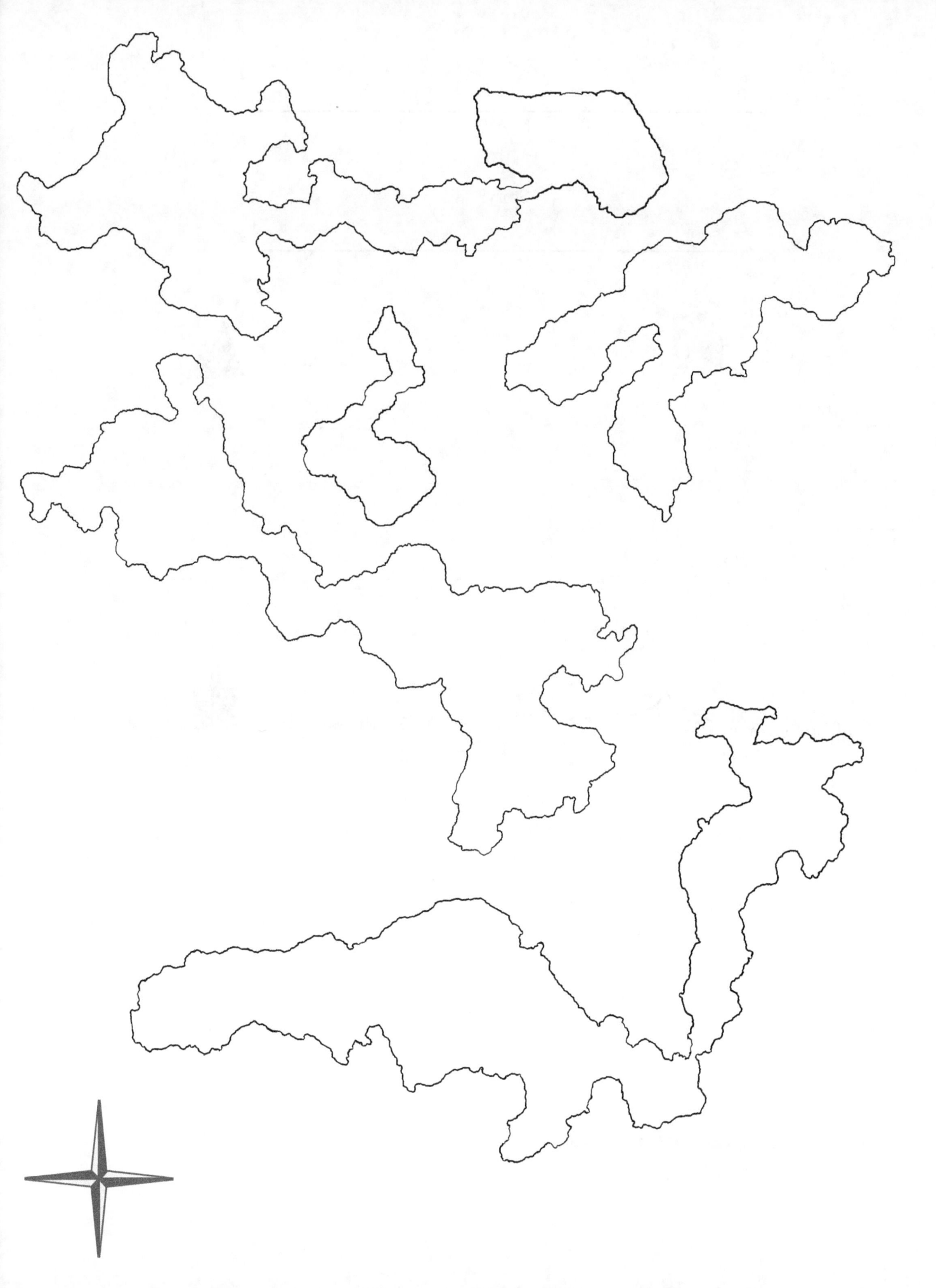

MAP

Story:

_____

Cities

_____
_____
_____
_____

Landmarks

_____
_____
_____
_____

Bodies of Water

_____
_____
_____
_____

Provinces/Districts

_____
_____
_____
_____

Lines and Symbols

Scale

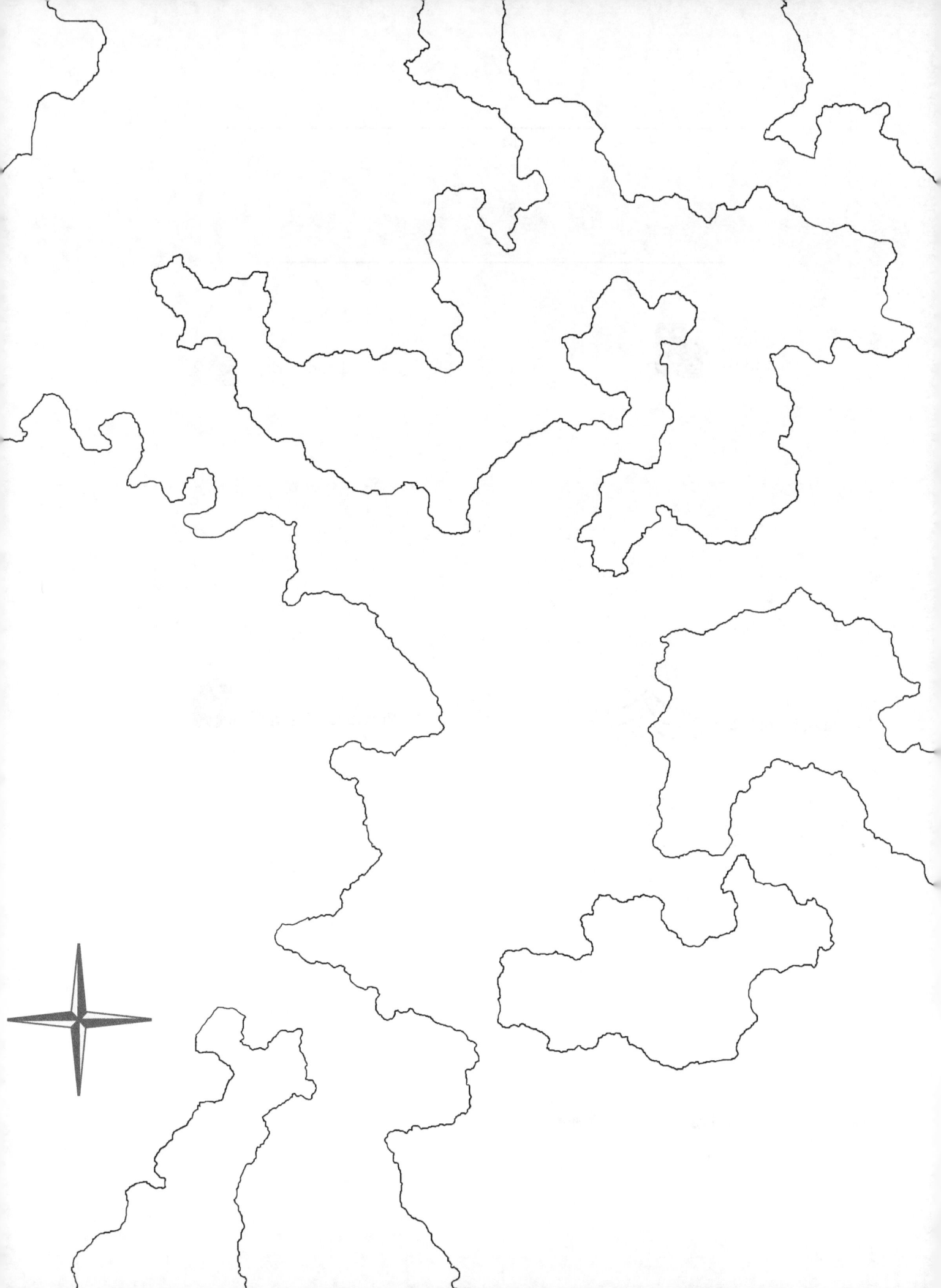

M A P

Story:

_____

Cities

Landmarks

_____
_____
_____
_____

_____
_____
_____
_____

Bodies of Water

Provinces/Districts

_____
_____
_____
_____

_____
_____
_____
_____

Lines and Symbols

Scale

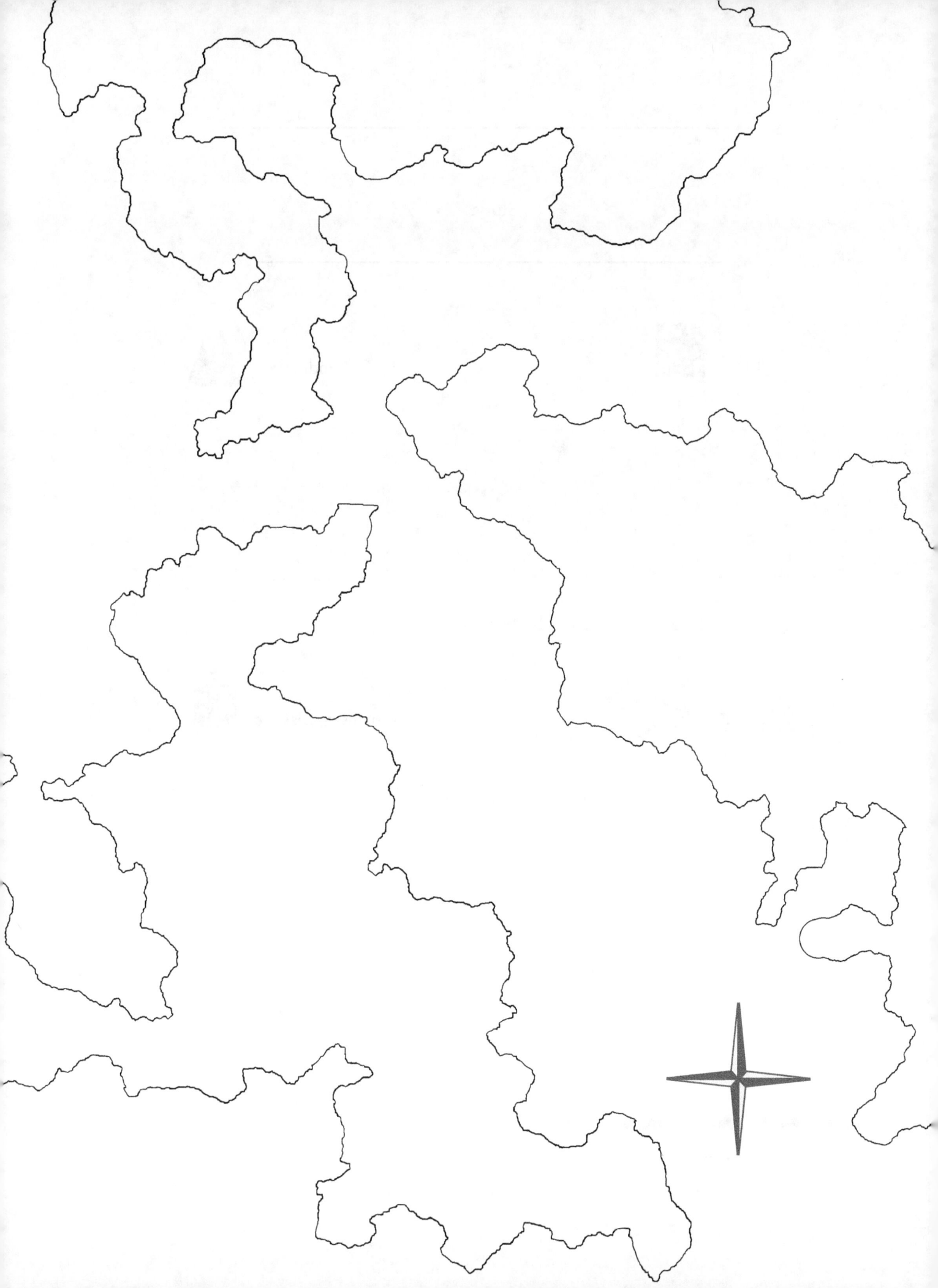

MAP

Story:

_____

Cities

_____
_____
_____
_____
_____

Landmarks

_____
_____
_____
_____
_____

Bodies of Water

_____
_____
_____
_____
_____

Provinces/Districts

_____
_____
_____
_____
_____

Lines and Symbols

Scale

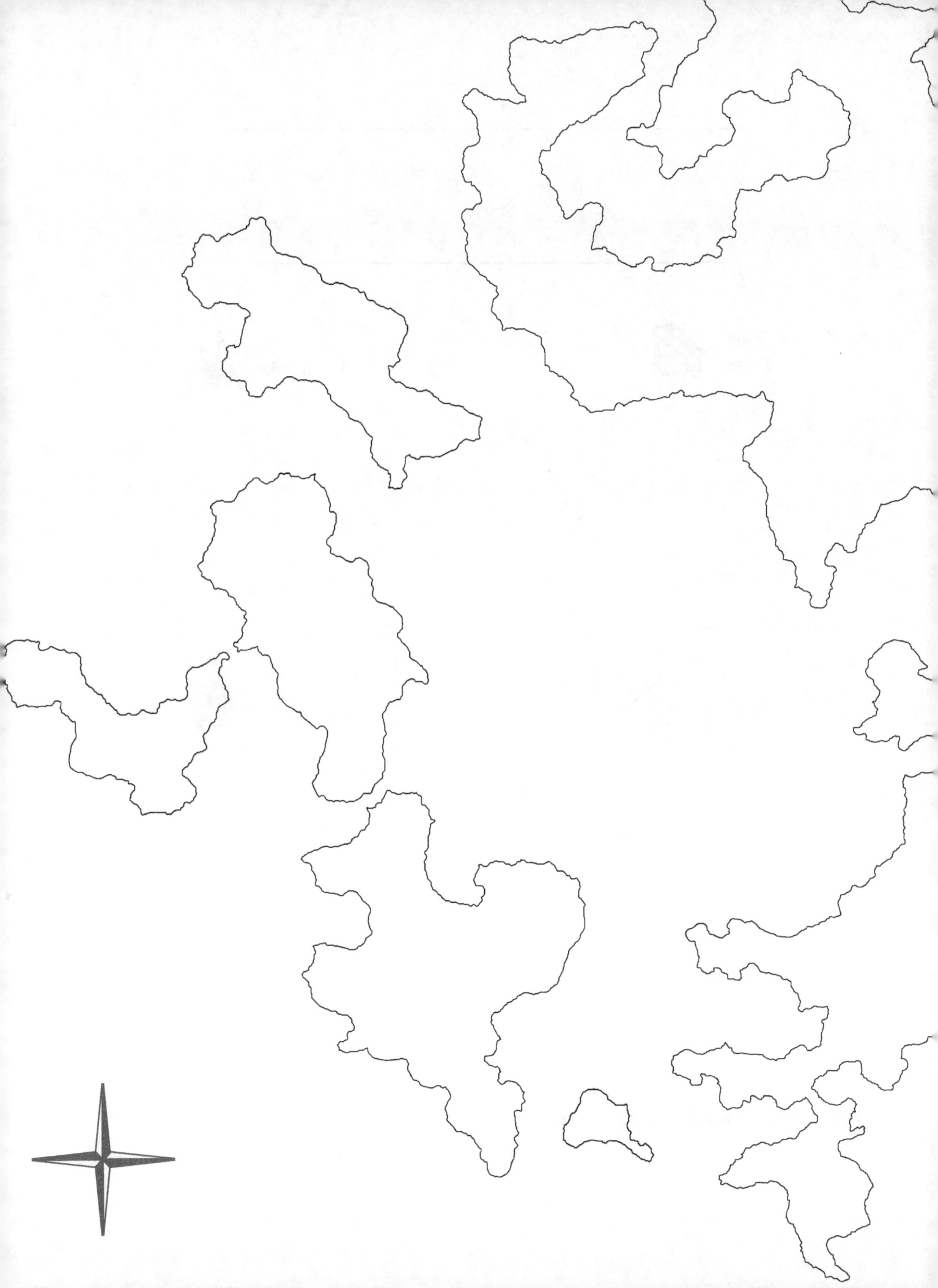

MAP

Story:

_____

Cities

_____
_____
_____
_____
_____

Landmarks

_____
_____
_____
_____
_____

Bodies of Water

_____
_____
_____
_____

Provinces/Districts

_____
_____
_____
_____

Lines and Symbols

Scale

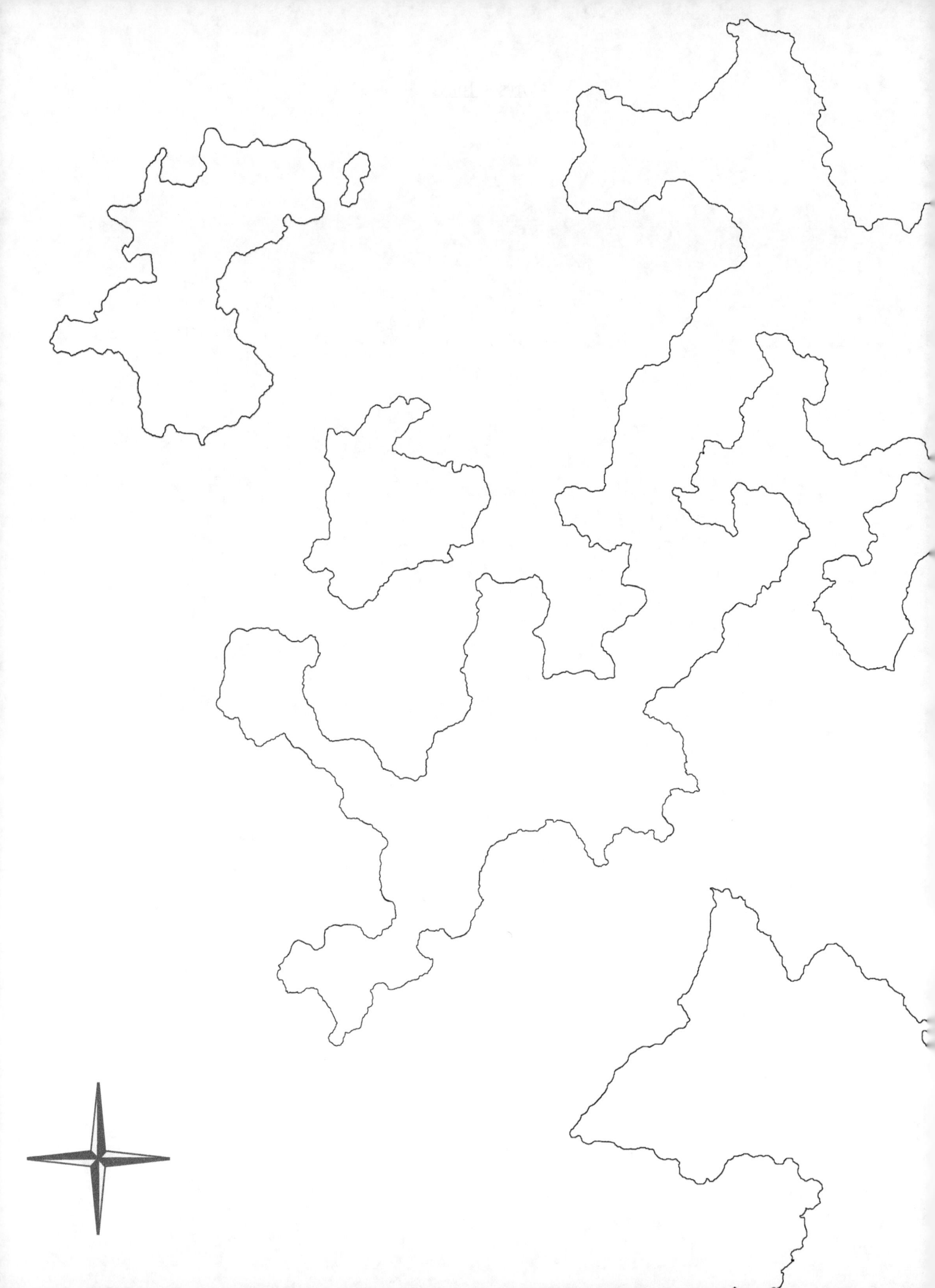

M A P

Story:

_____

Cities

Landmarks

_____
_____
_____
_____
_____

_____
_____
_____
_____
_____

Bodies of Water

Provinces/Districts

_____
_____
_____
_____

_____
_____
_____
_____

Lines and Symbols

Scale

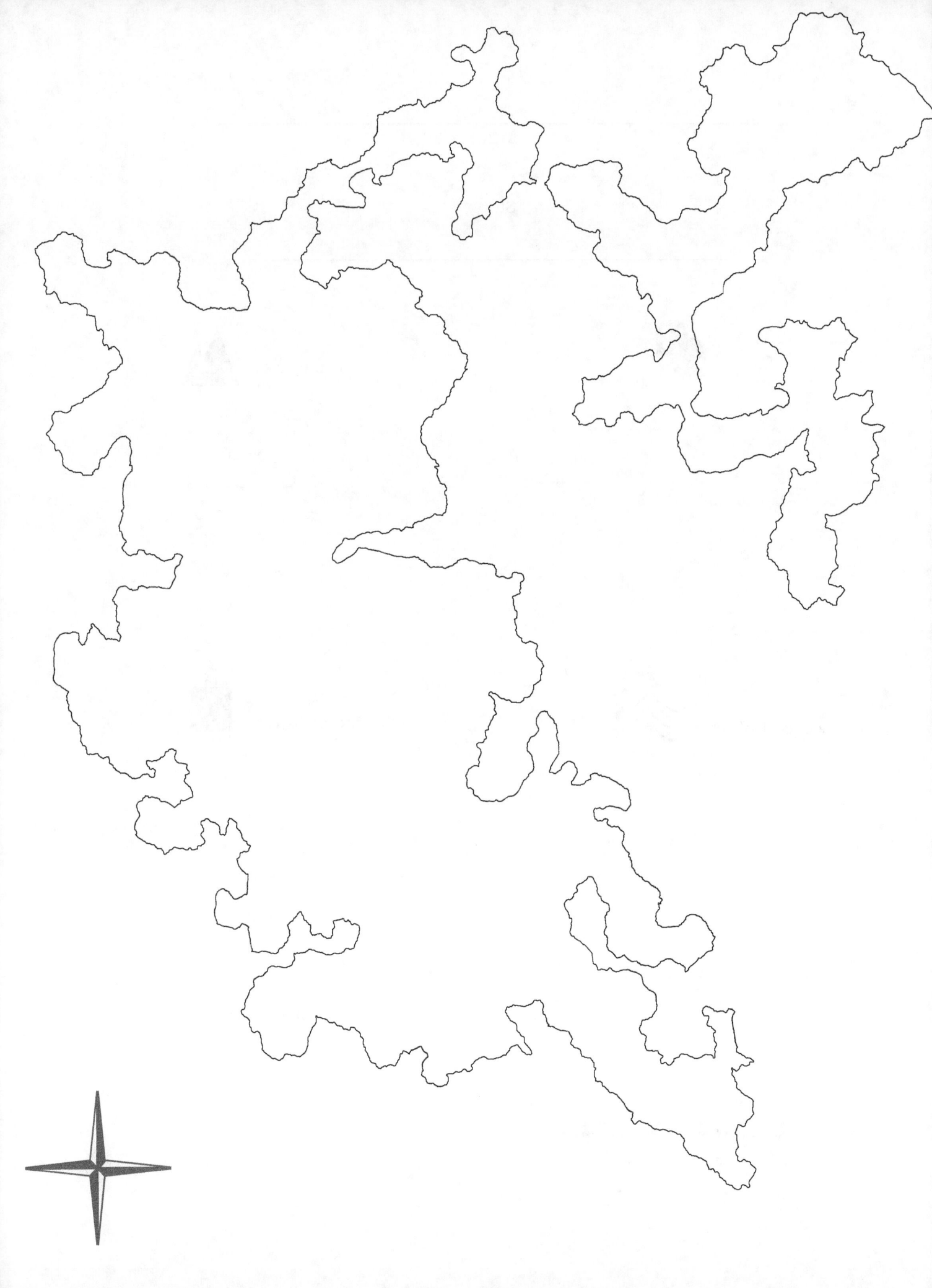

M A P

Story:

_____

Cities

_____
_____
_____
_____

Landmarks

_____
_____
_____
_____

Bodies of Water

_____
_____
_____
_____

Provinces/Districts

_____
_____
_____
_____

Lines and Symbols

Scale

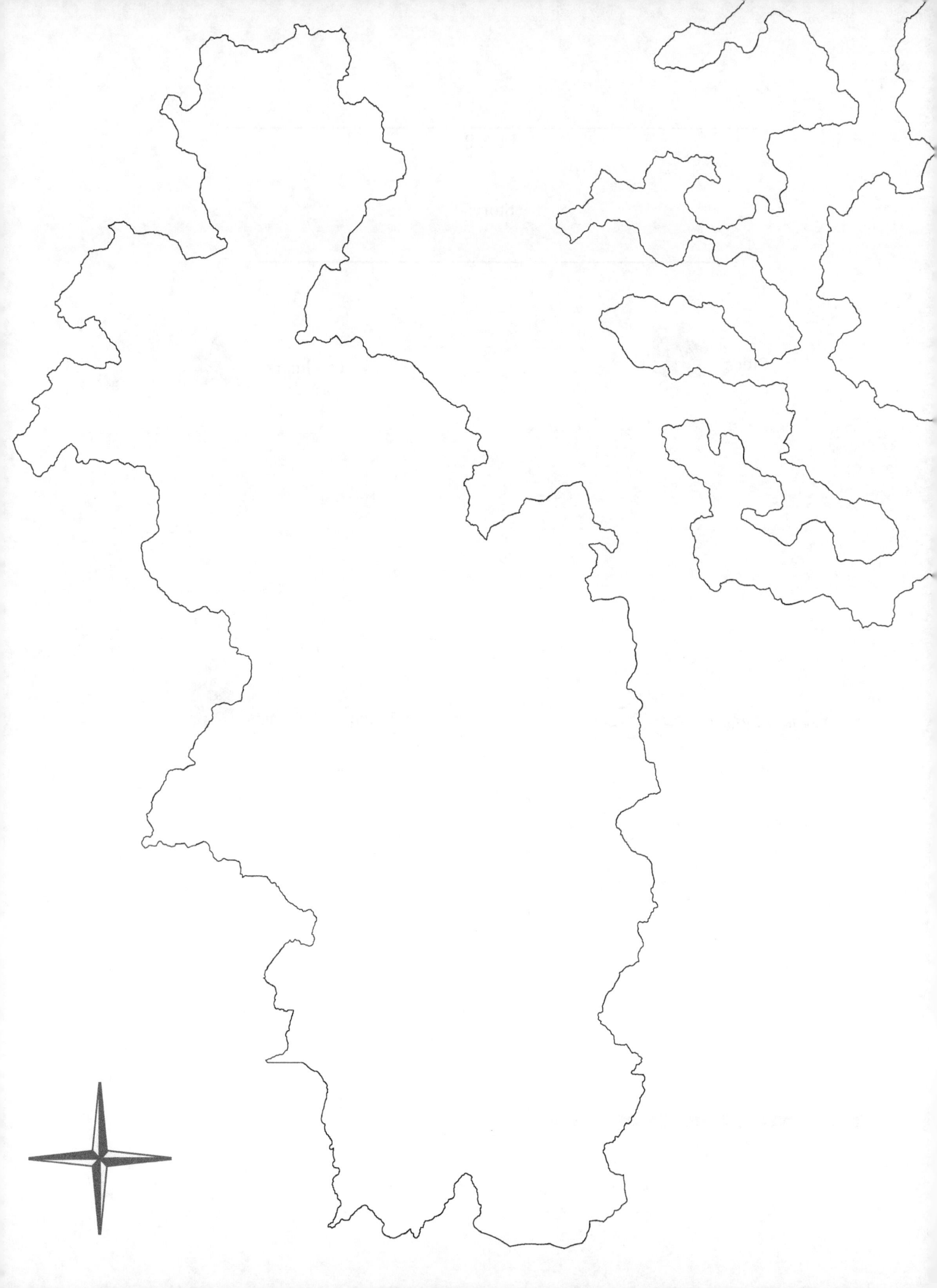

MAP

Story:

_____

Cities

Landmarks

Bodies of Water

Provinces/Districts

Lines and Symbols

Scale

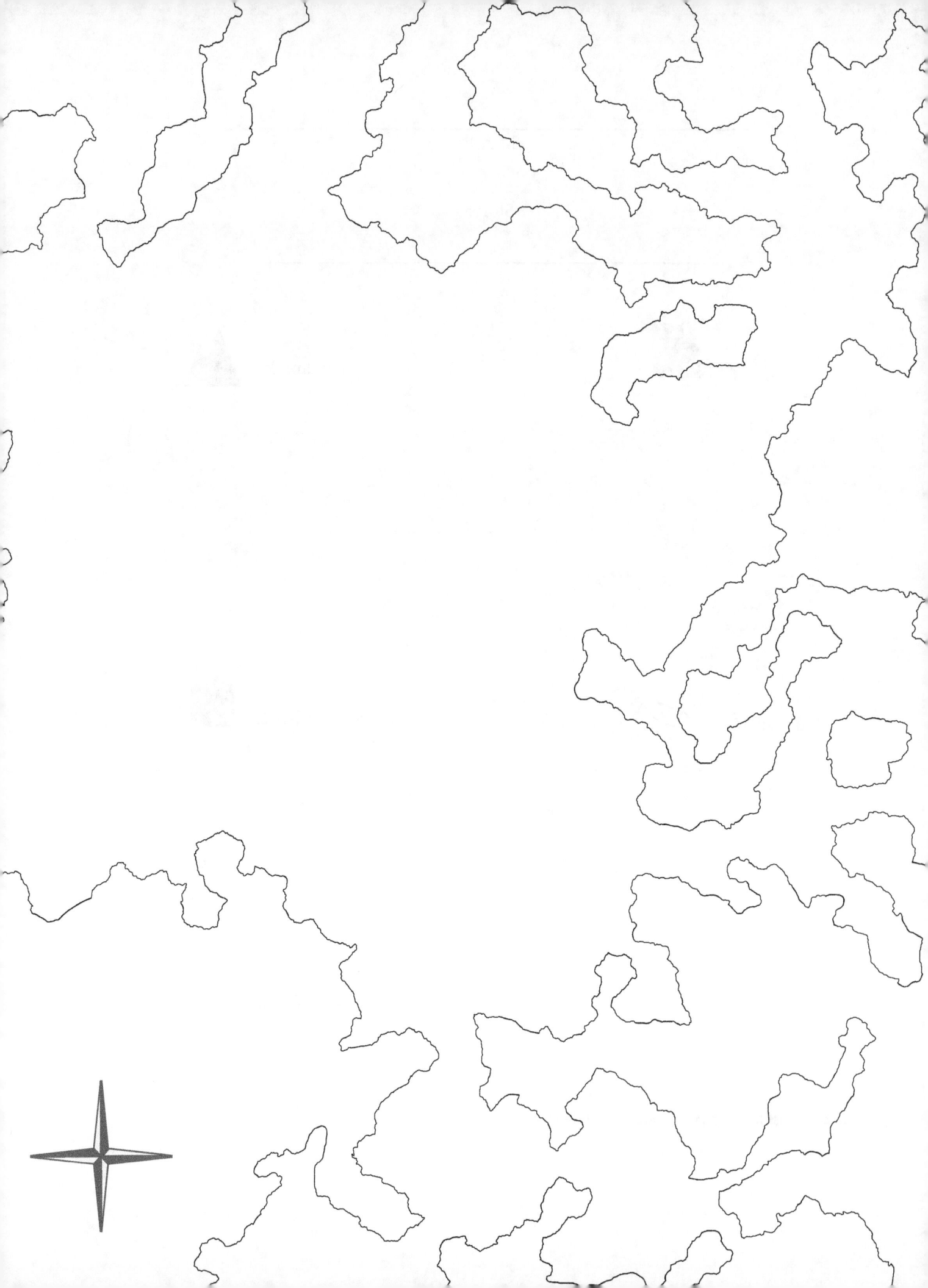

MAP

Story:

_____

Cities

Landmarks

Bodies of Water

Provinces/Districts

Lines and Symbols

Scale

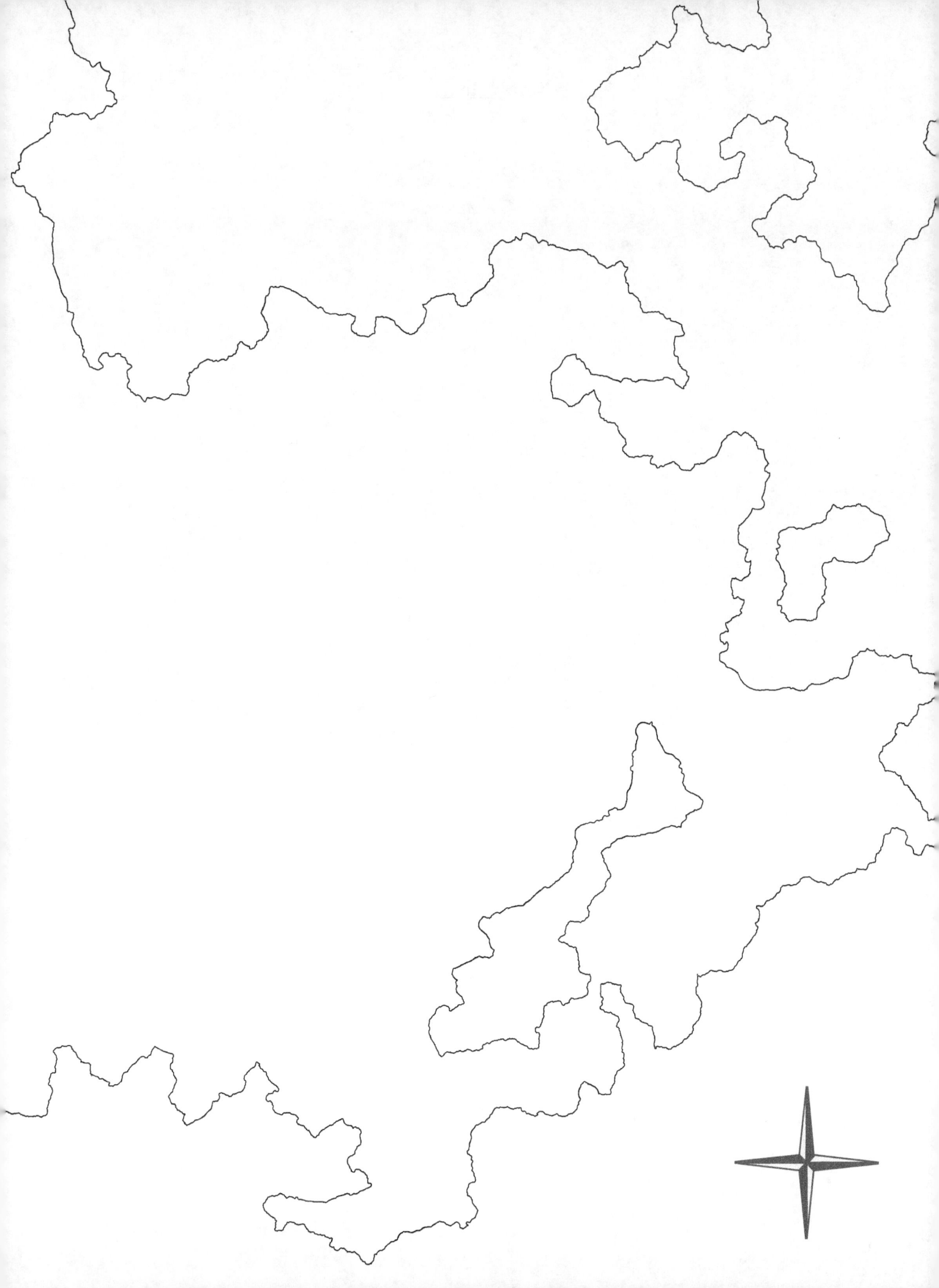

NOTES & IDEAS

M A P

Story:

_____

Cities

Landmarks

Bodies of Water

Provinces/Districts

Lines and Symbols

Scale

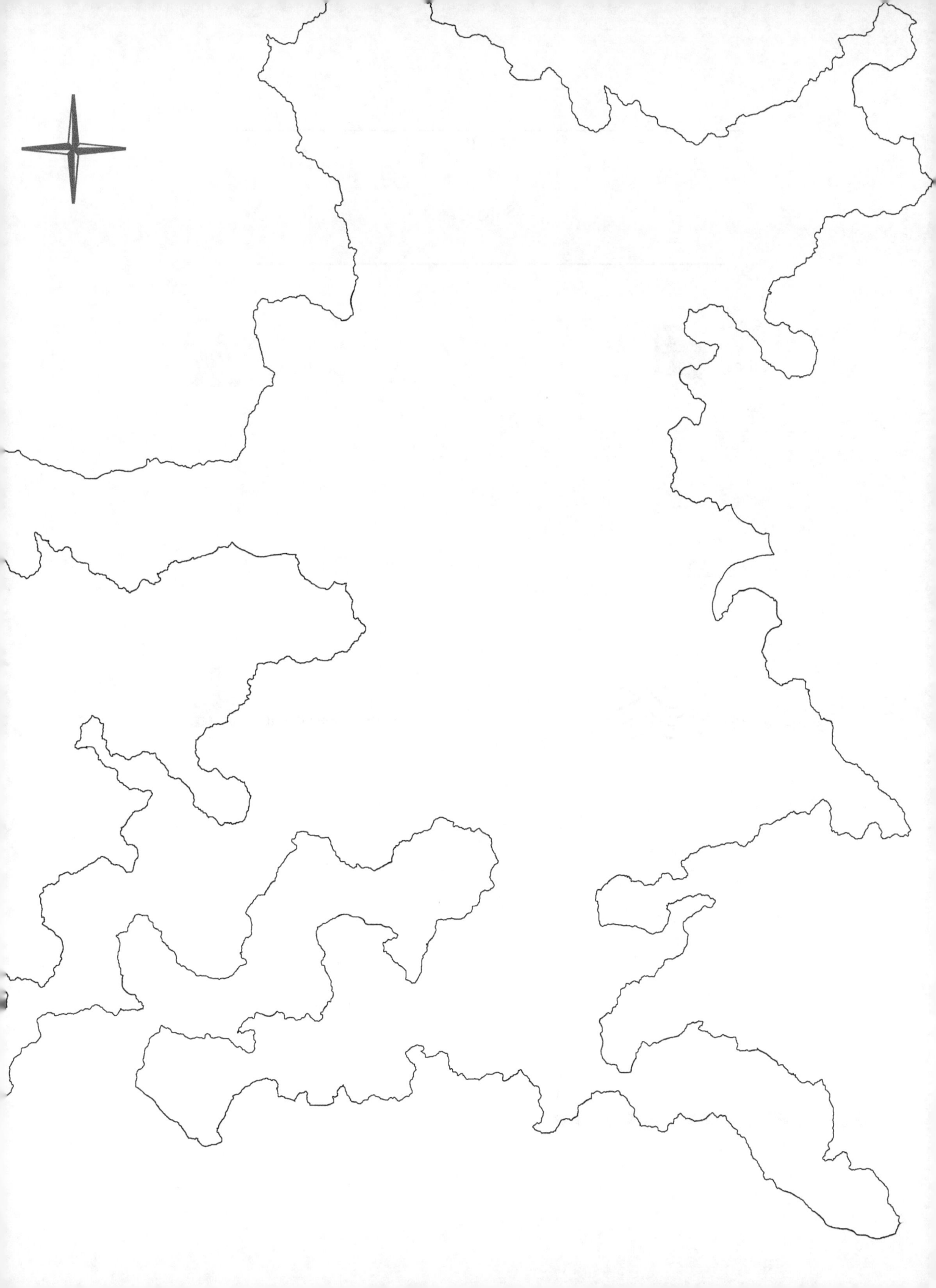

M A P

Story:

_____

Cities

Landmarks

Bodies of Water

Provinces/Districts

Lines and Symbols

Scale

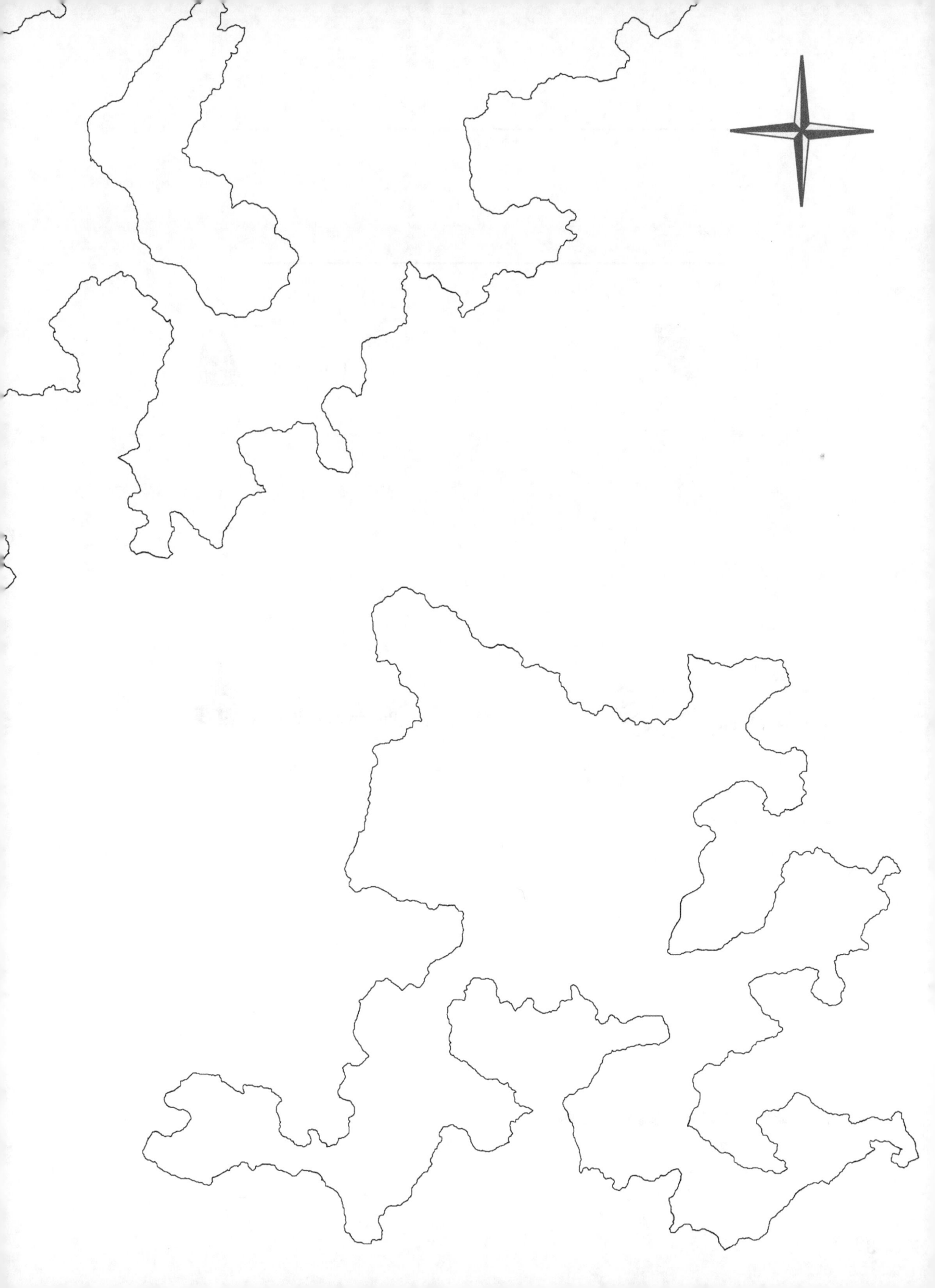

MAP

Story:

_____

Cities

Landmarks

Bodies of Water

Provinces/Districts

Lines and Symbols

Scale

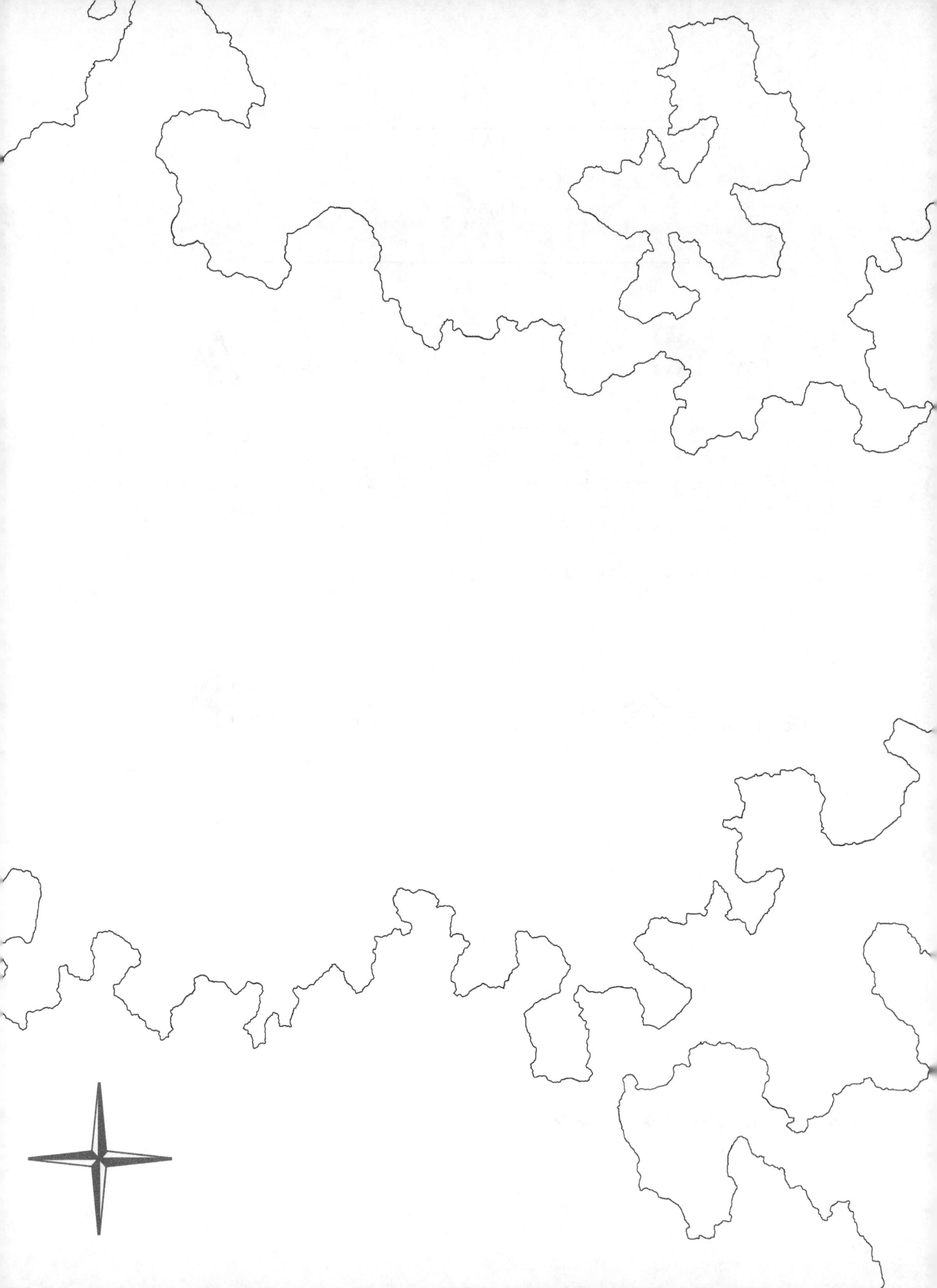

M A P

Story:

_____

Cities

_____
_____
_____
_____
_____

Landmarks

_____
_____
_____
_____
_____

Bodies of Water

_____
_____
_____
_____

Provinces/Districts

_____
_____
_____
_____

Lines and Symbols

Scale

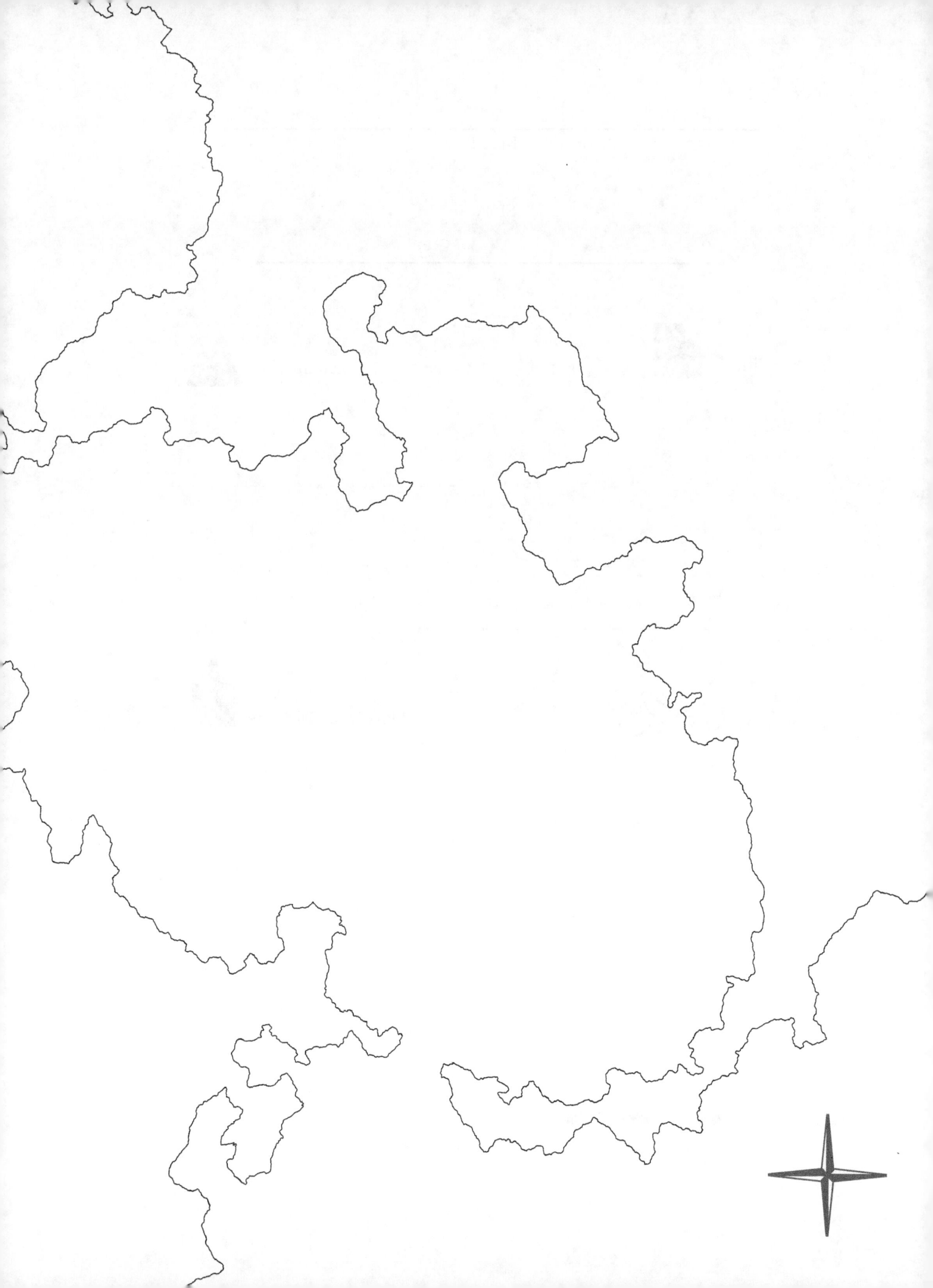

M A P

Story:

_____

Cities

_____
_____
_____
_____
_____

Landmarks

_____
_____
_____
_____
_____

Bodies of Water

_____
_____
_____
_____

Provinces/Districts

_____
_____
_____
_____

Lines and Symbols

Scale

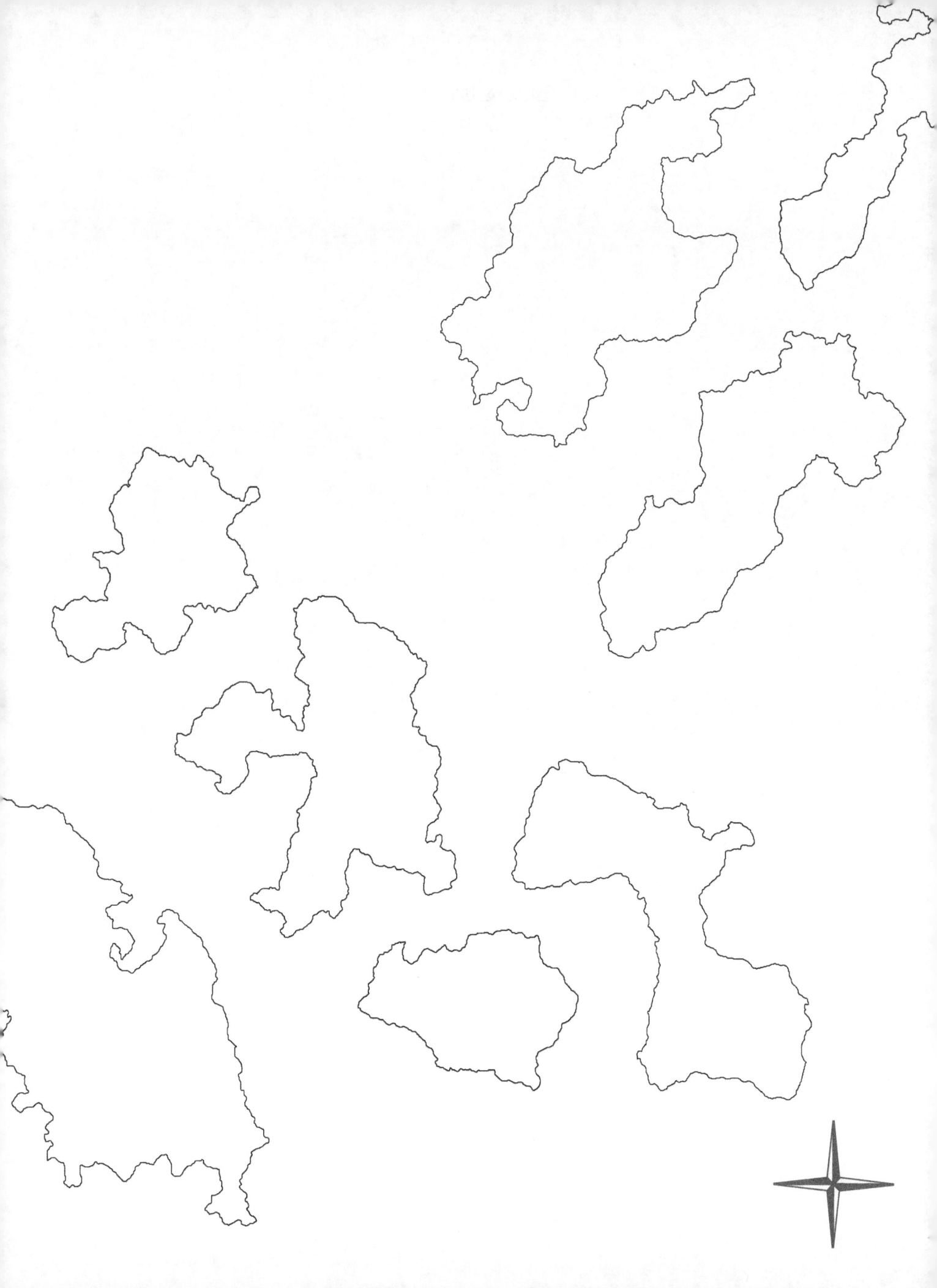

MAP

Story:

_____

Cities

_____
_____
_____
_____
_____

Landmarks

_____
_____
_____
_____
_____

Bodies of Water

_____
_____
_____
_____
_____

Provinces/Districts

_____
_____
_____
_____
_____

Lines and Symbols

Scale

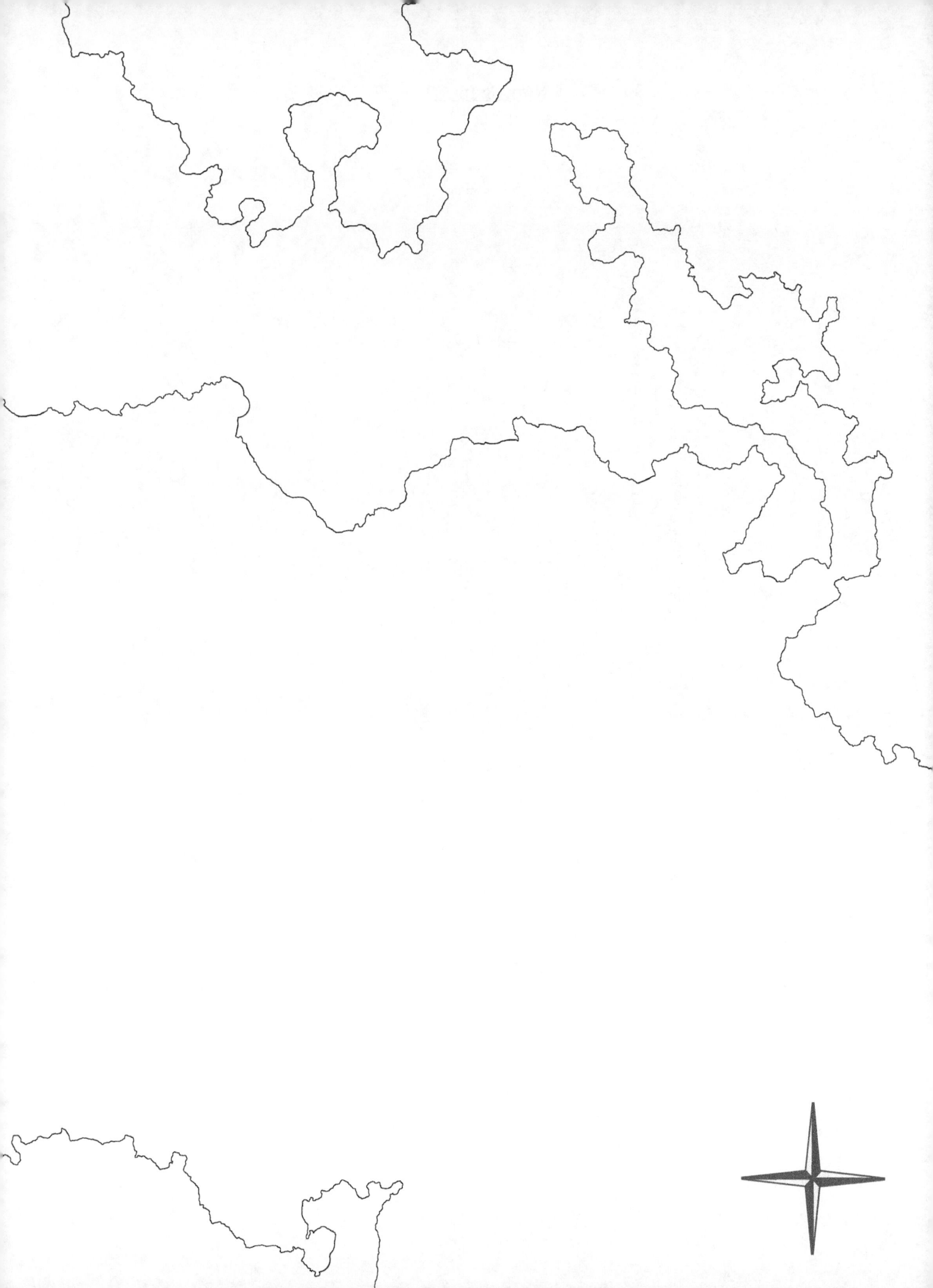

MAP

Story:

_____

Cities

Landmarks

Bodies of Water

Provinces/Districts

Lines and Symbols

Scale

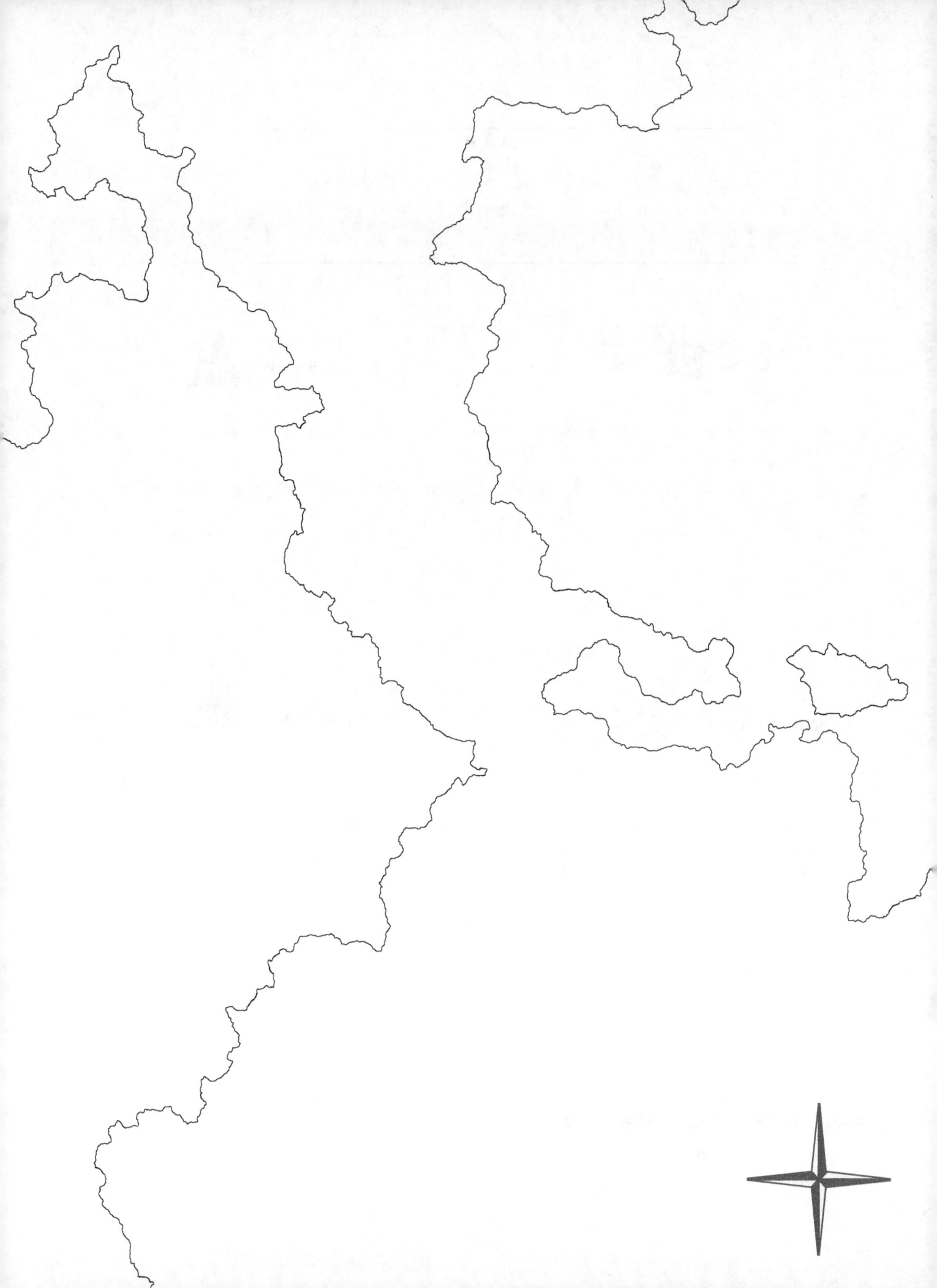

M A P

Story:

_____

Cities

_____
_____
_____
_____

Landmarks

_____
_____
_____
_____

Bodies of Water

_____
_____
_____
_____

Provinces/Districts

_____
_____
_____
_____

Lines and Symbols

Scale

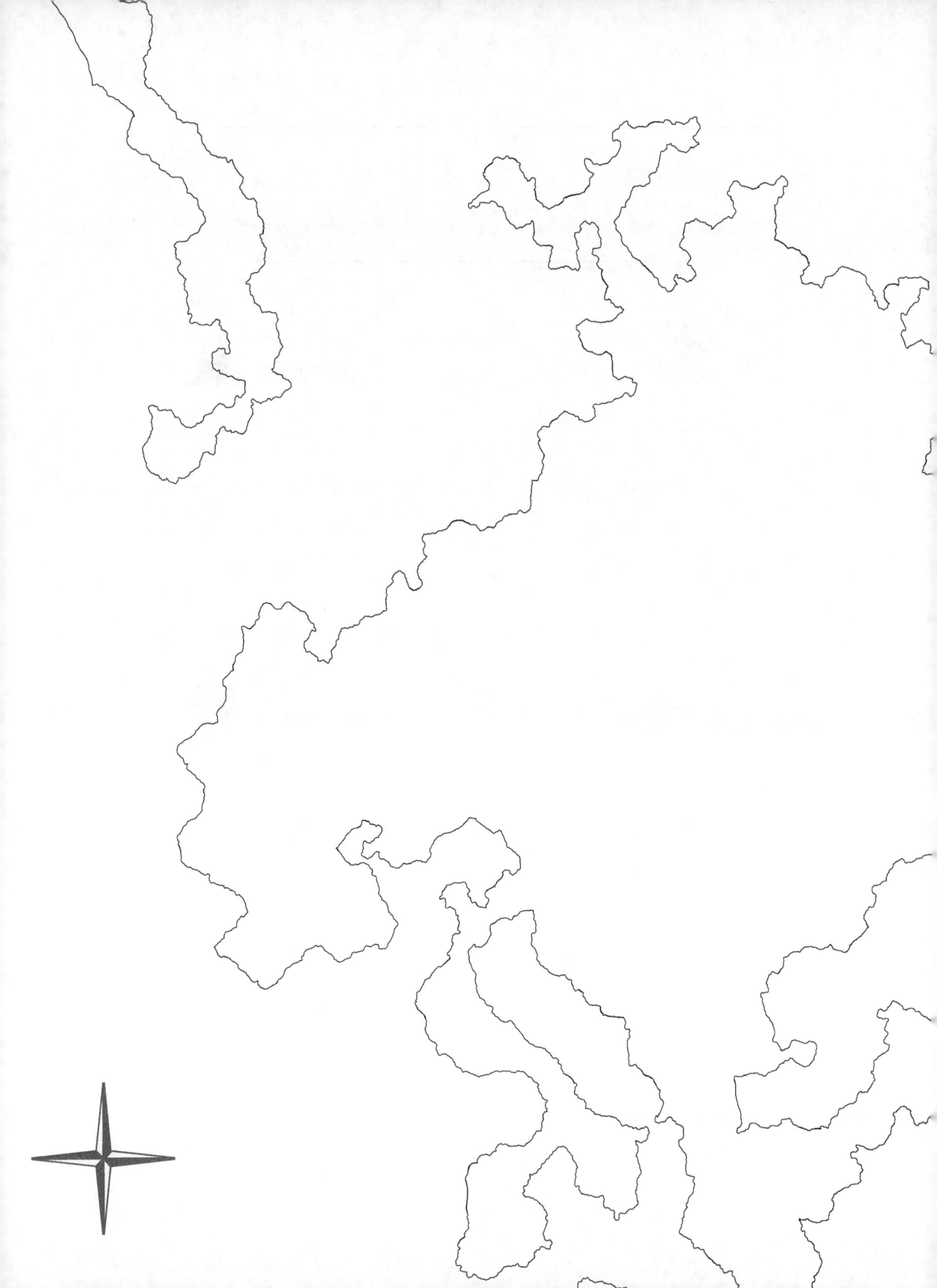

MAP

Story:

_____

Cities

Landmarks

Bodies of Water

Provinces/Districts

Lines and Symbols

Scale

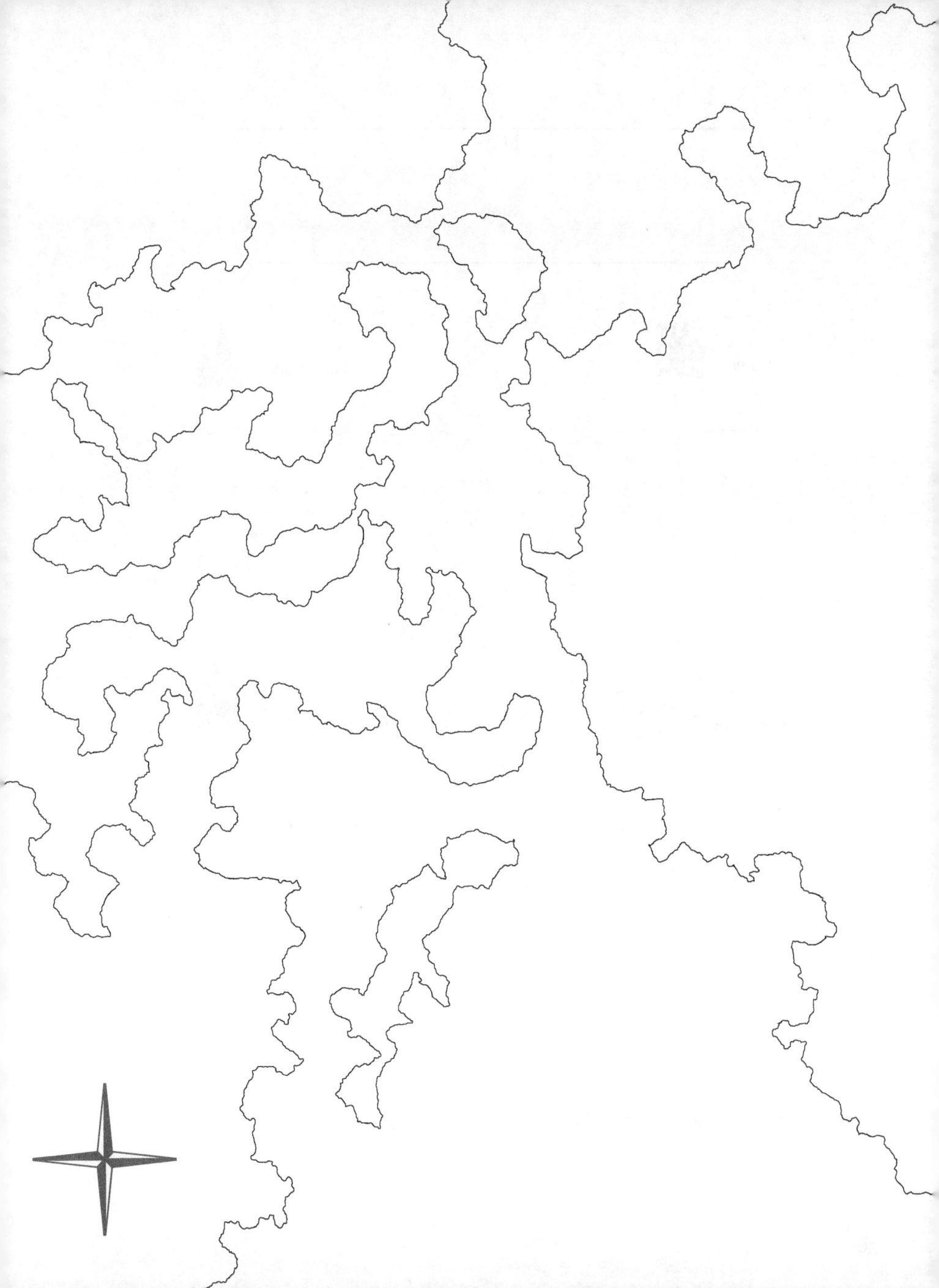

M A P

Story:

_____

Cities

Landmarks

_____
_____
_____
_____
_____

Bodies of Water

Provinces/Districts

_____
_____
_____
_____

Lines and Symbols

Scale

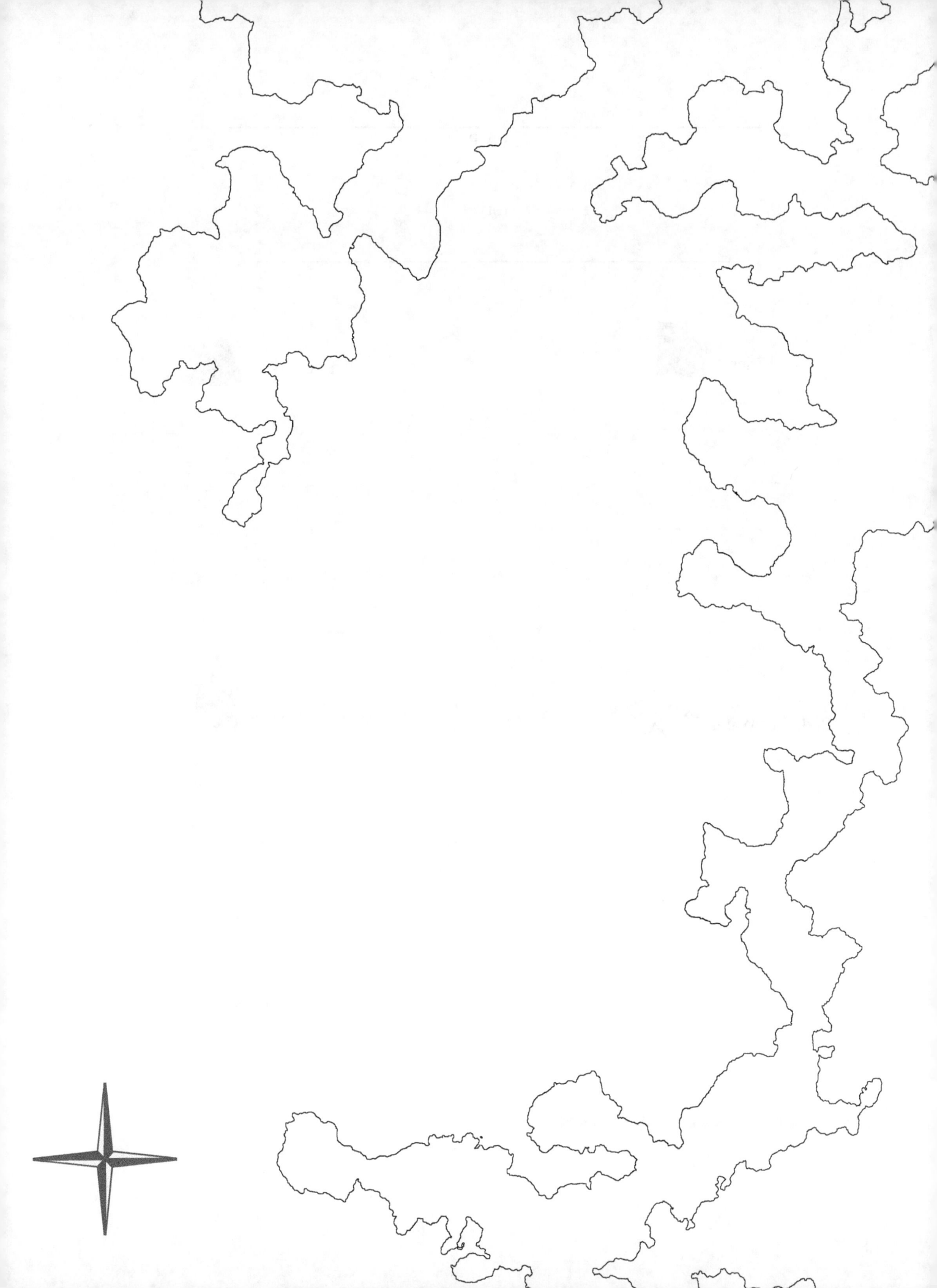

M A P

Story:

_____

Cities

_____
_____
_____
_____

Landmarks

_____
_____
_____
_____

Bodies of Water

_____
_____
_____
_____

Provinces/Districts

_____
_____
_____
_____

Lines and Symbols

Scale

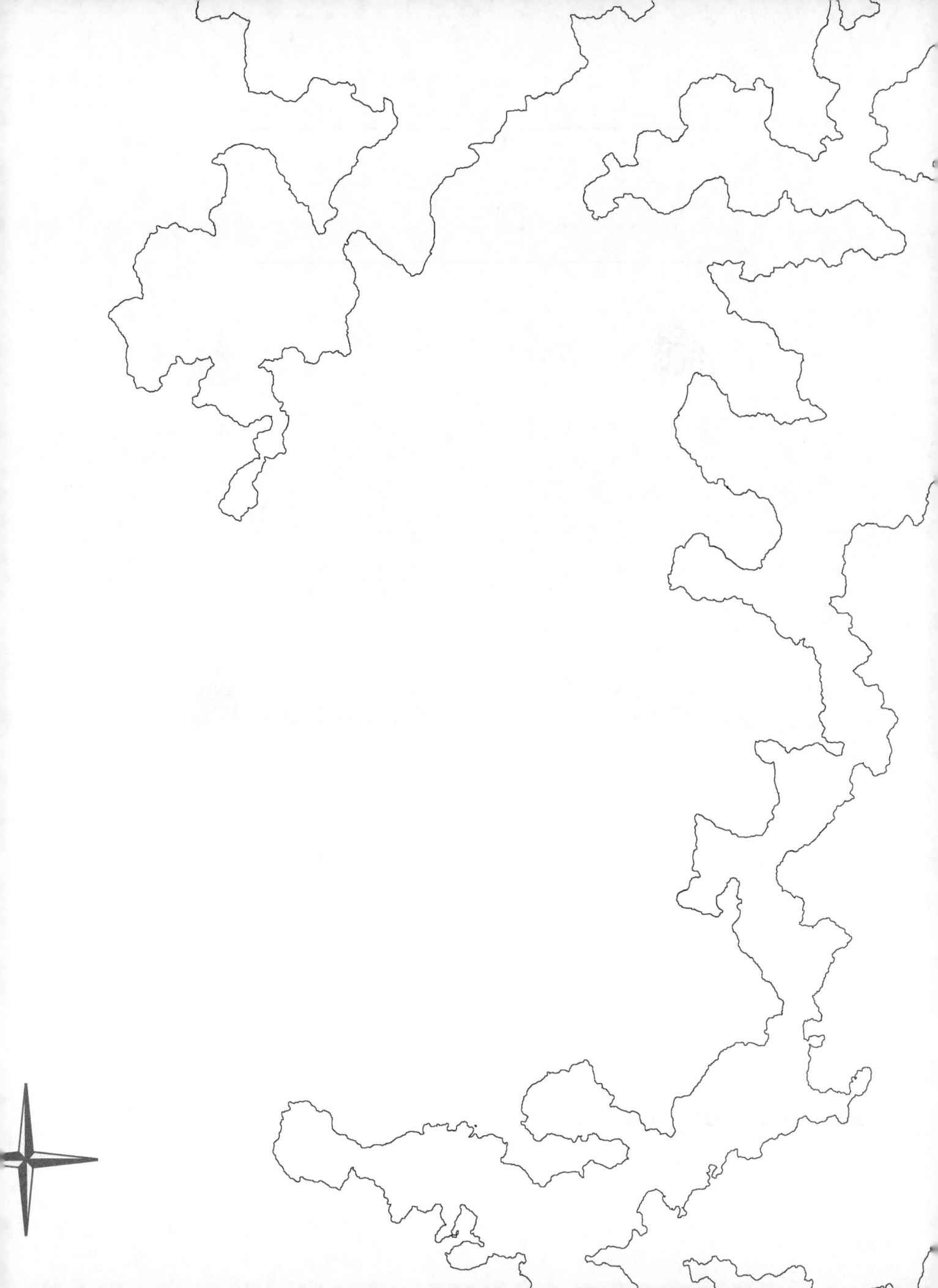

MAP

Story:

_____

Cities

Landmarks

_____
_____
_____
_____
_____

Bodies of Water

Provinces/Districts

_____
_____
_____
_____

Lines and Symbols

Scale

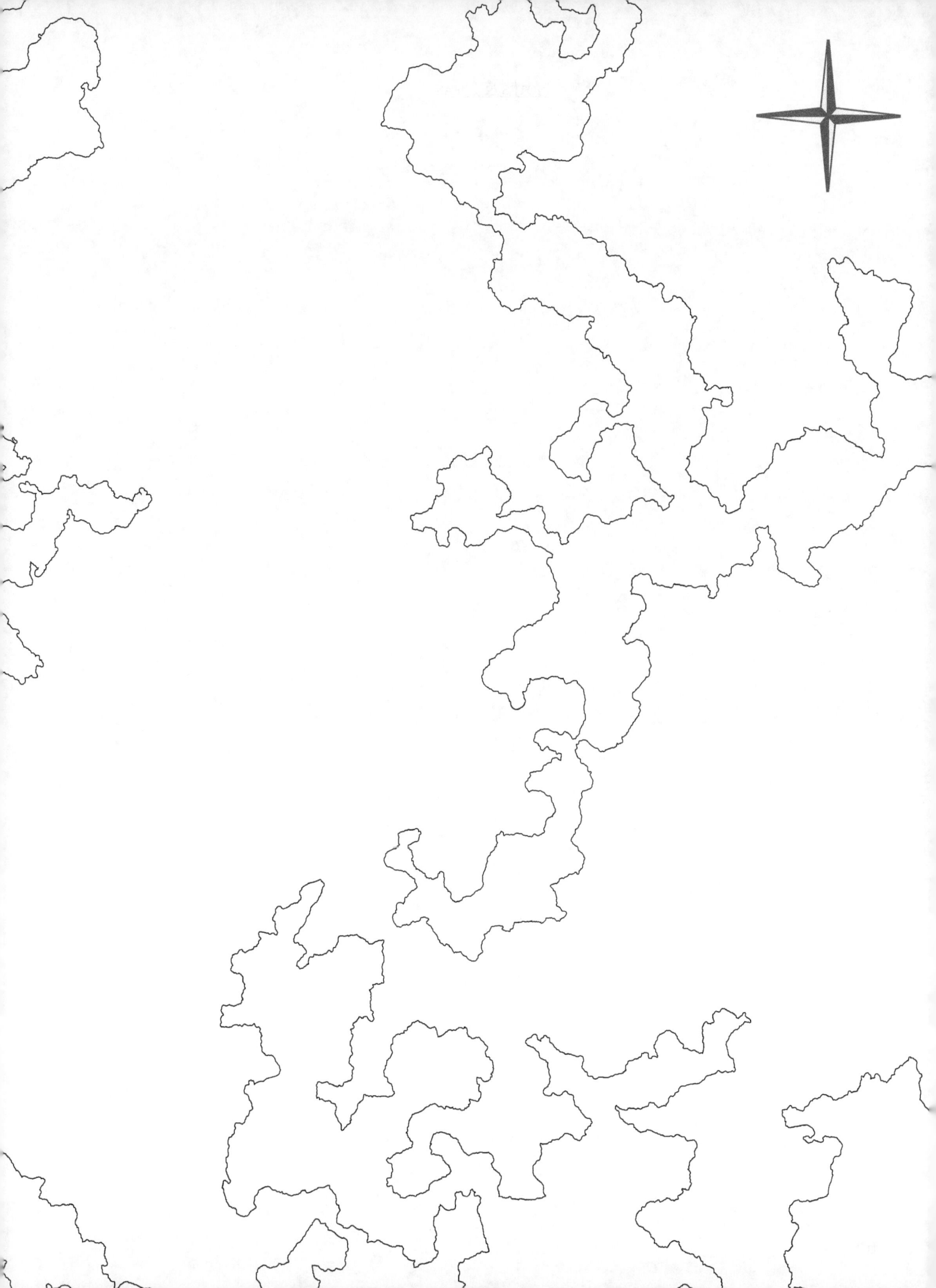

Story:

_____

Cities

Landmarks

_____
_____
_____
_____
_____

_____
_____
_____
_____
_____

Bodies of Water

Provinces/Districts

_____
_____
_____
_____
_____

_____
_____
_____
_____
_____

Lines and Symbols

Scale

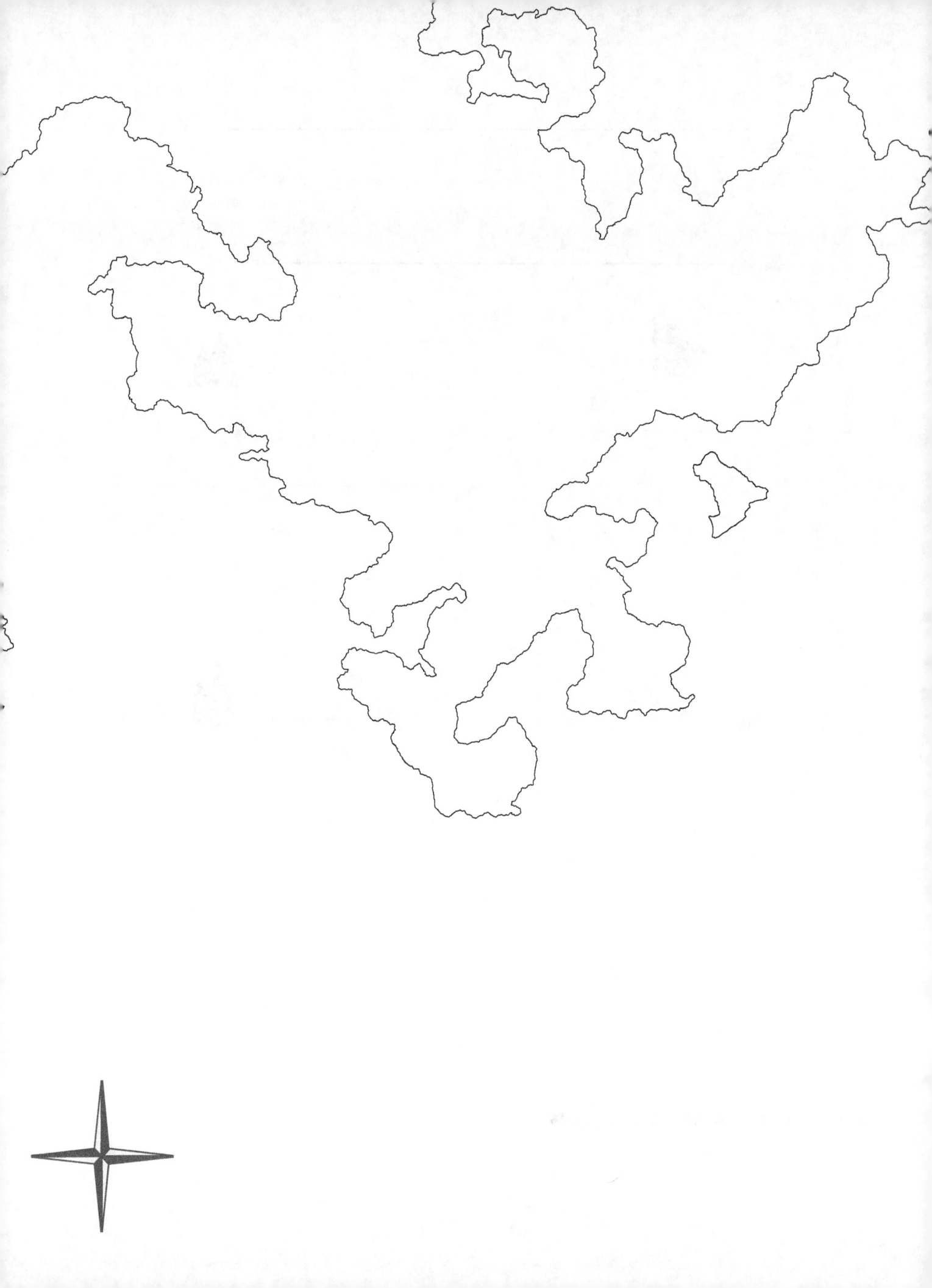

MAP

Story:

_____

Cities

_____
_____
_____
_____

Landmarks

_____
_____
_____
_____

Bodies of Water

_____
_____
_____
_____

Provinces/Districts

_____
_____
_____
_____

Lines and Symbols

Scale

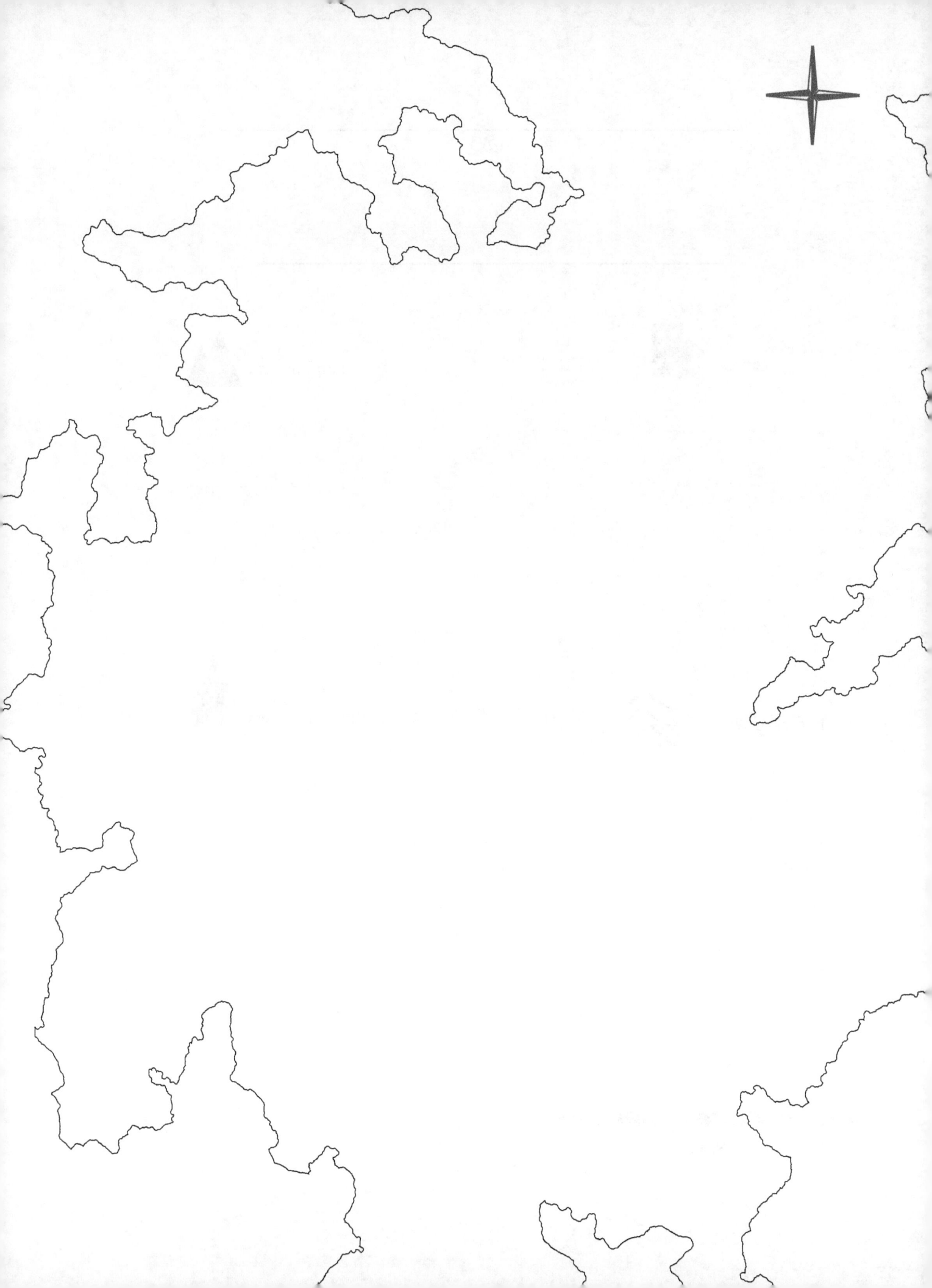

MAP

Story:

_____

Cities

Landmarks

_____
_____
_____
_____

Bodies of Water

Provinces/Districts

_____
_____
_____
_____

Lines and Symbols

Scale

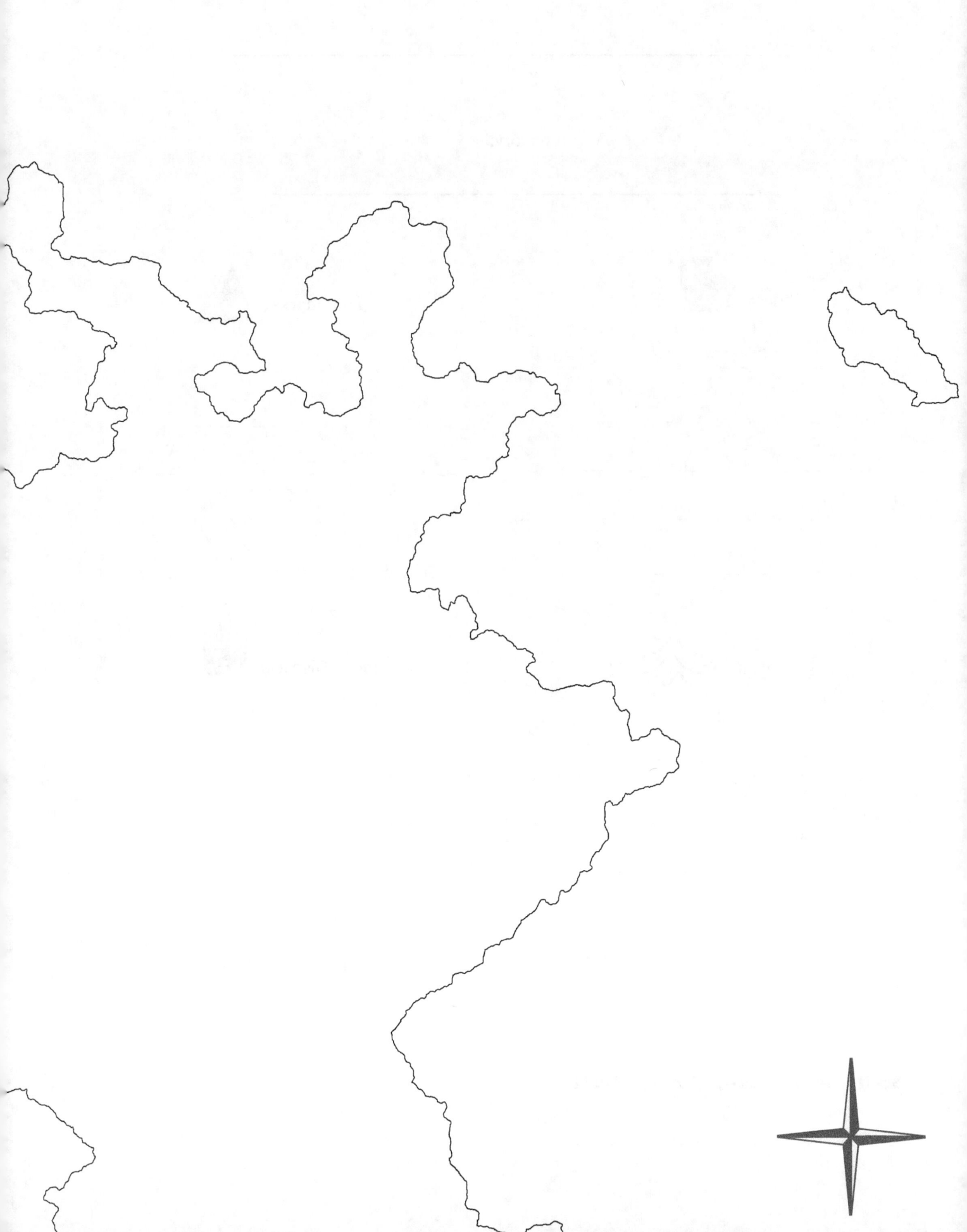

MAP

Story:

_____

Cities

Landmarks

_____
_____
_____
_____

_____
_____
_____
_____

Bodies of Water

Provinces/Districts

_____
_____
_____
_____

_____
_____
_____
_____

Lines and Symbols

Scale

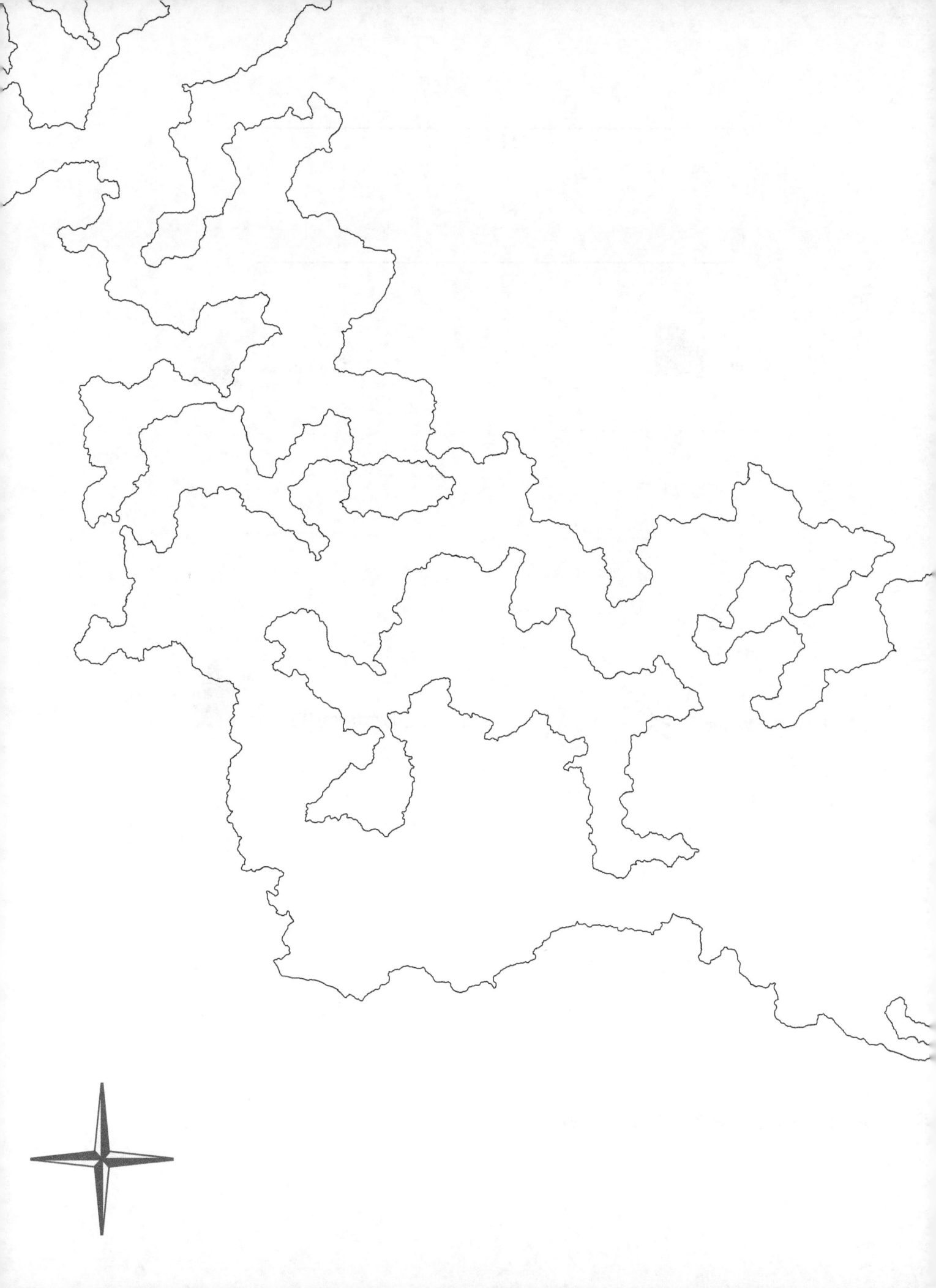

M A P

Story:

_____

Cities

Landmarks

_____
_____
_____
_____

_____
_____
_____
_____

Bodies of Water

Provinces/Districts

_____
_____
_____
_____

_____
_____
_____
_____

Lines and Symbols

Scale

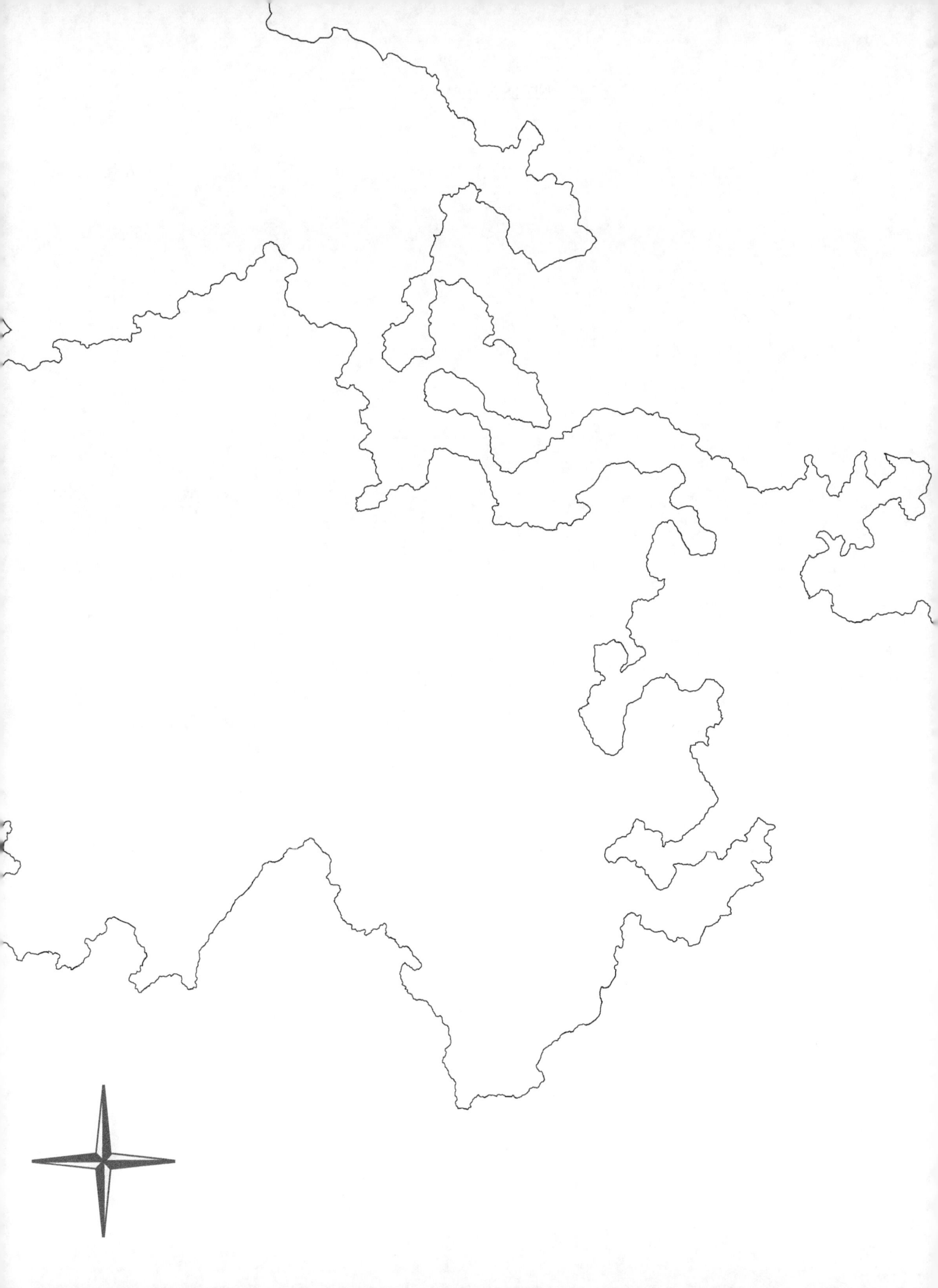

MAP

Story:

_____

Cities

Landmarks

_____
_____
_____
_____

_____
_____
_____
_____

Bodies of Water

Provinces/Districts

_____
_____
_____
_____

_____
_____
_____
_____

Lines and Symbols

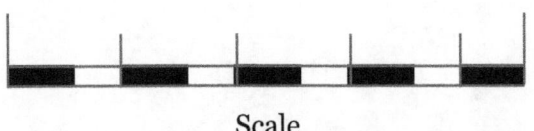

Scale

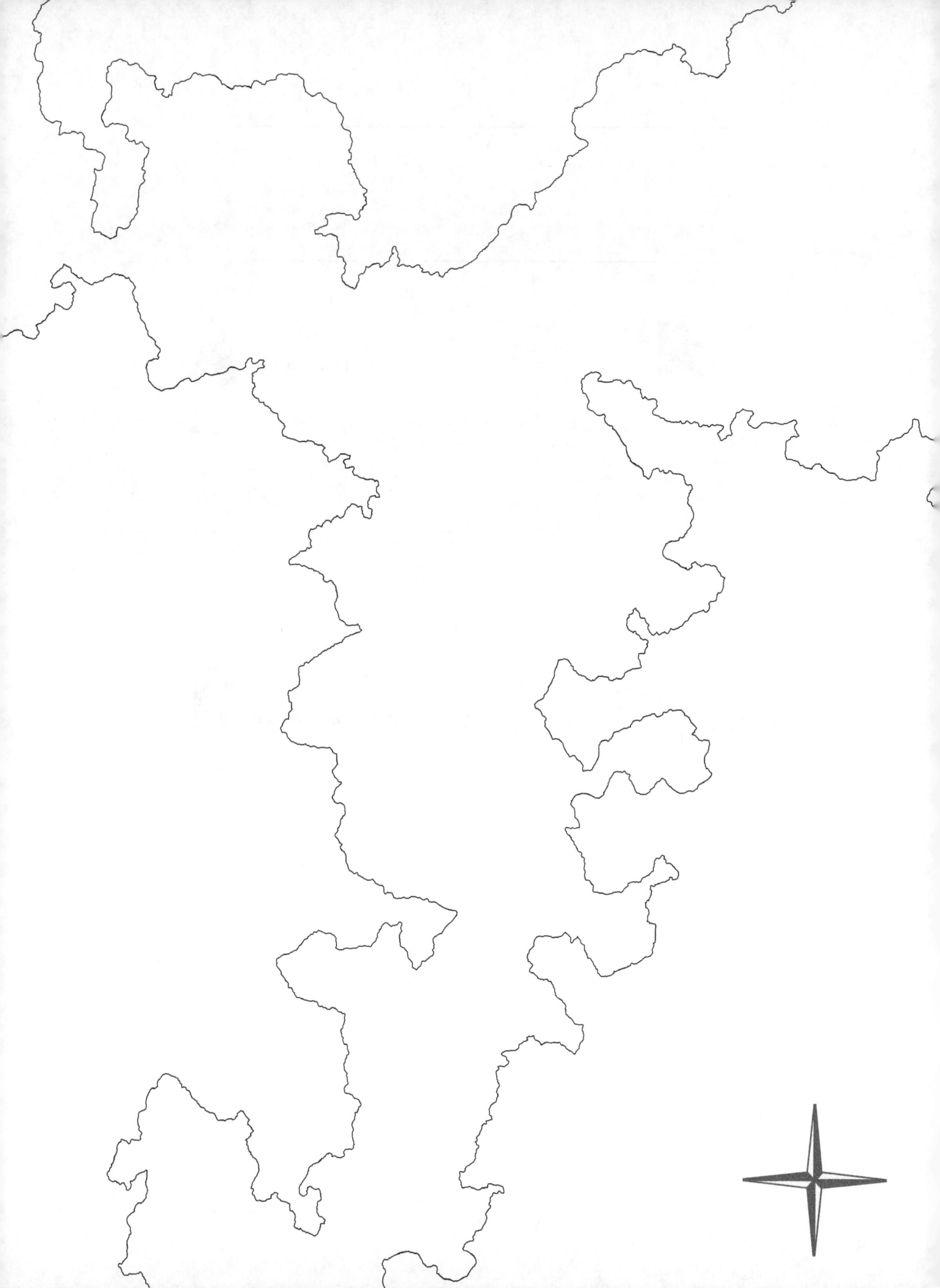

MAP

Story:

_____

Cities

_____
_____
_____
_____

Landmarks

_____
_____
_____
_____

Bodies of Water

_____
_____
_____
_____

Provinces/Districts

_____
_____
_____
_____

Lines and Symbols

Scale

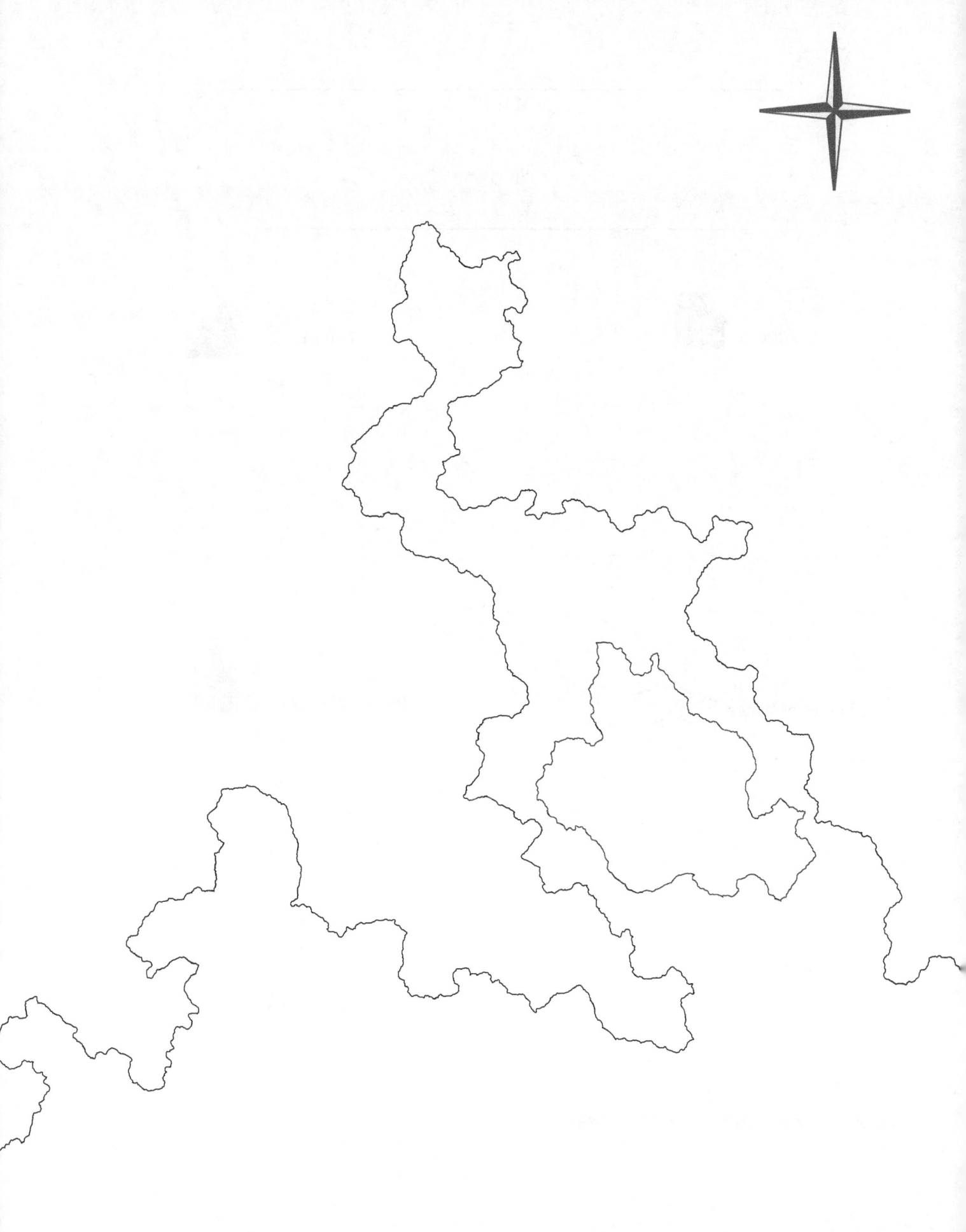

MAP

Story:

_____

Cities

Landmarks

Bodies of Water

Provinces/Districts

Lines and Symbols

Scale

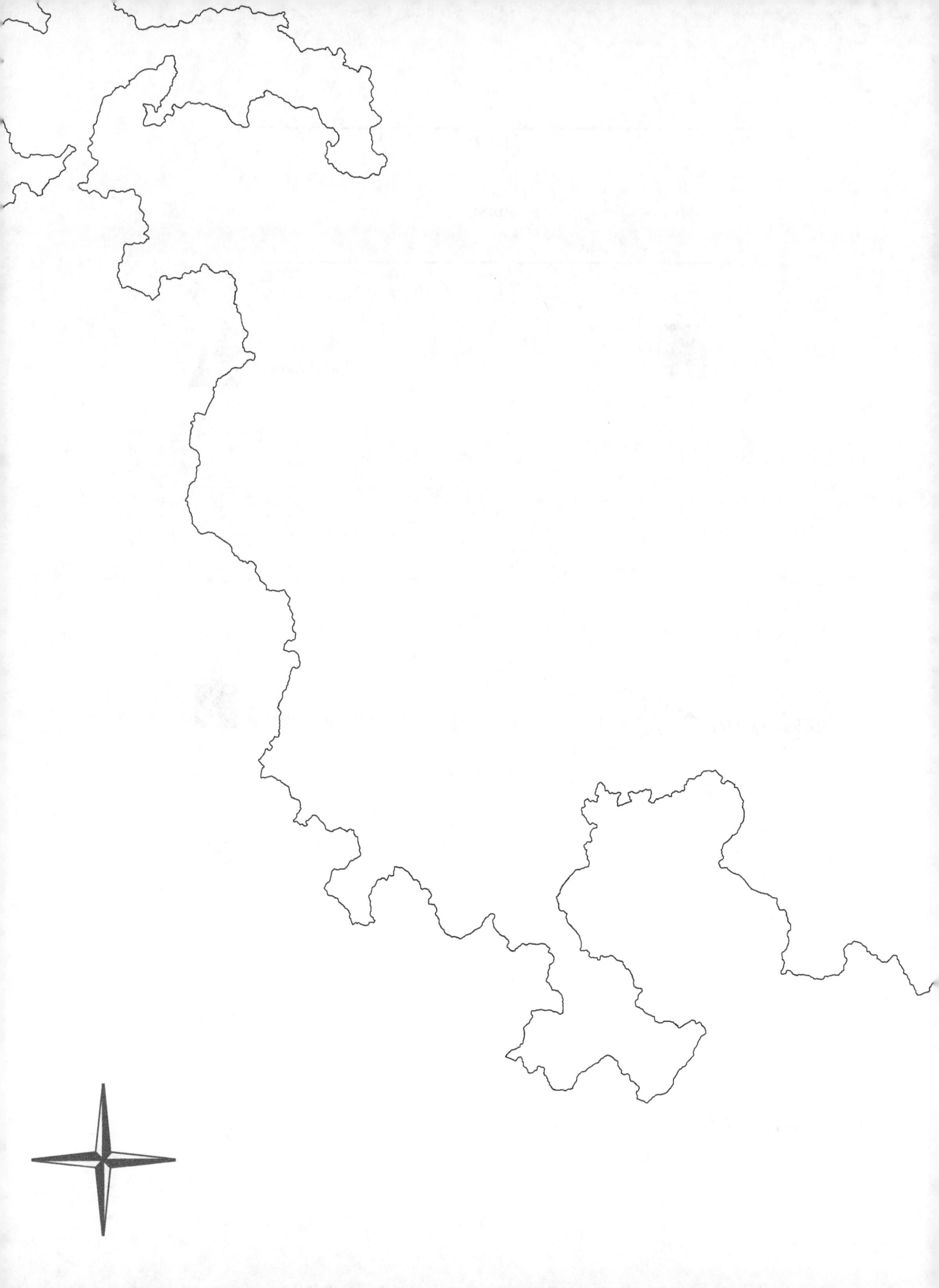

M A P

Story:

_____

Cities

Landmarks

_____
_____
_____
_____
_____

Bodies of Water

Provinces/Districts

_____
_____
_____
_____

Lines and Symbols

Scale

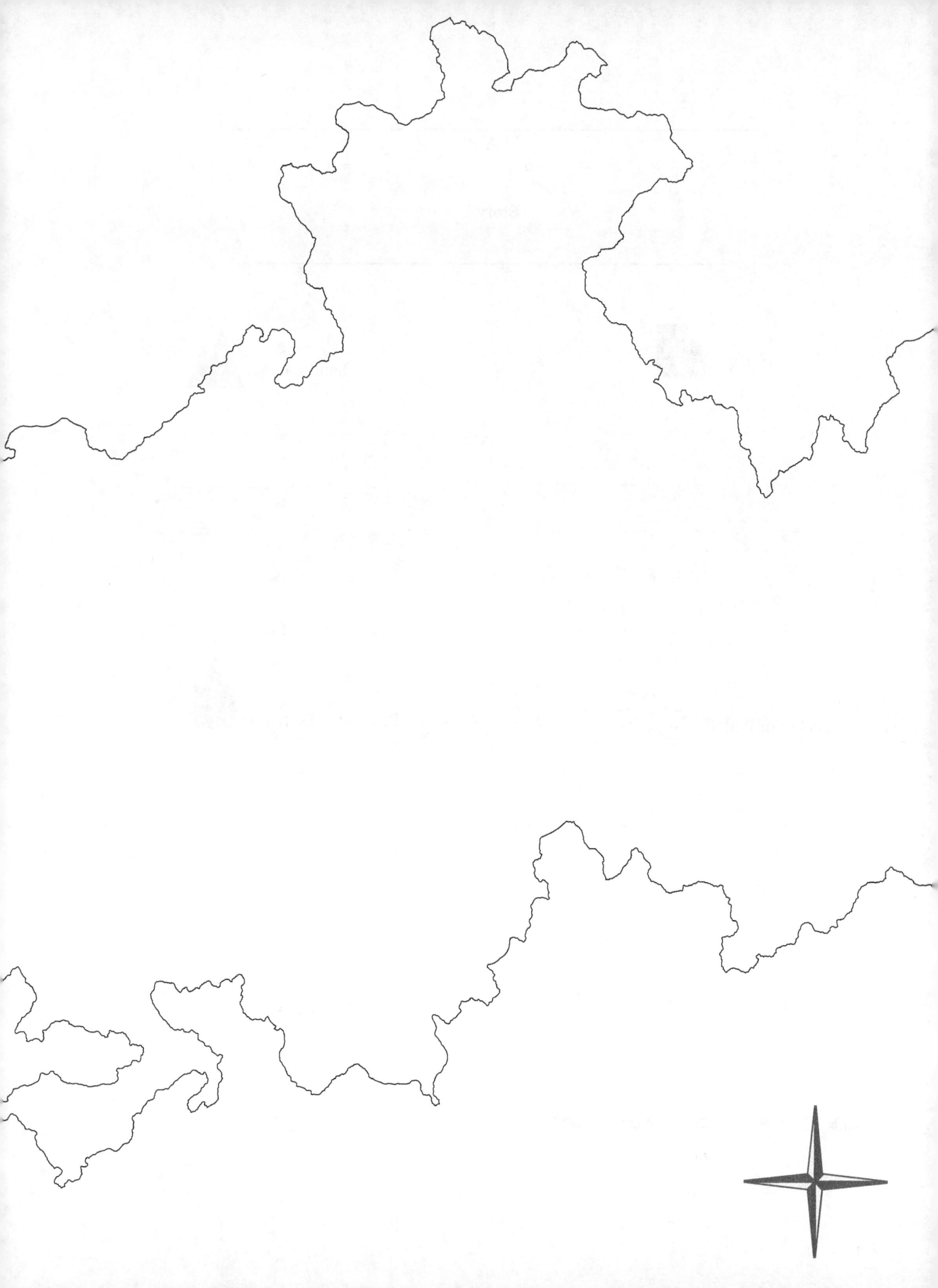

M A P

Story:

_____

Cities

Landmarks

_____
_____
_____
_____
_____

_____
_____
_____
_____
_____

Bodies of Water

Provinces/Districts

_____
_____
_____
_____
_____

_____
_____
_____
_____
_____

Lines and Symbols

Scale

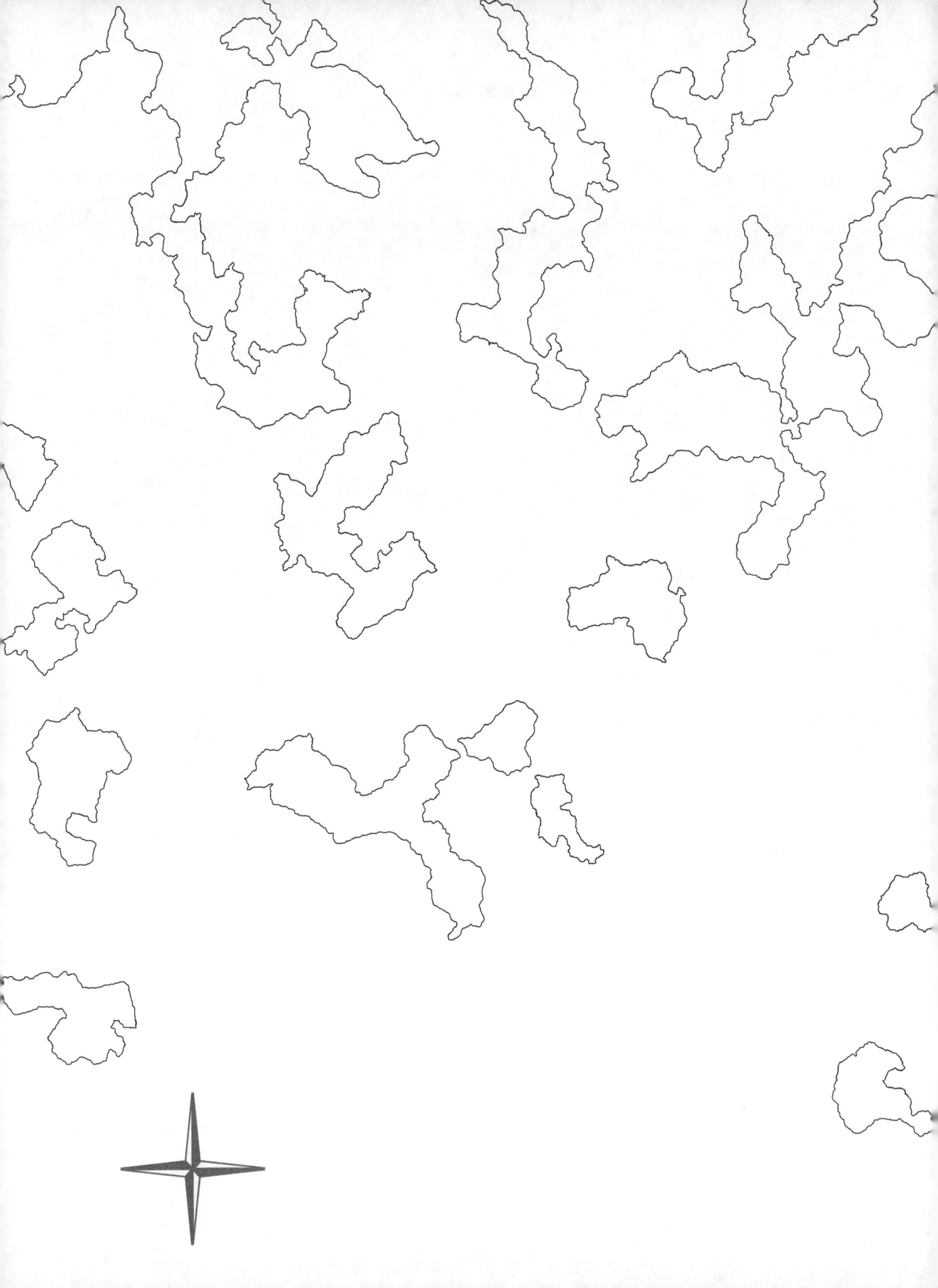

MAP

Story:

_____

Cities

_____
_____
_____
_____

Landmarks

_____
_____
_____
_____

Bodies of Water

_____
_____
_____
_____

Provinces/Districts

_____
_____
_____
_____

Lines and Symbols

Scale

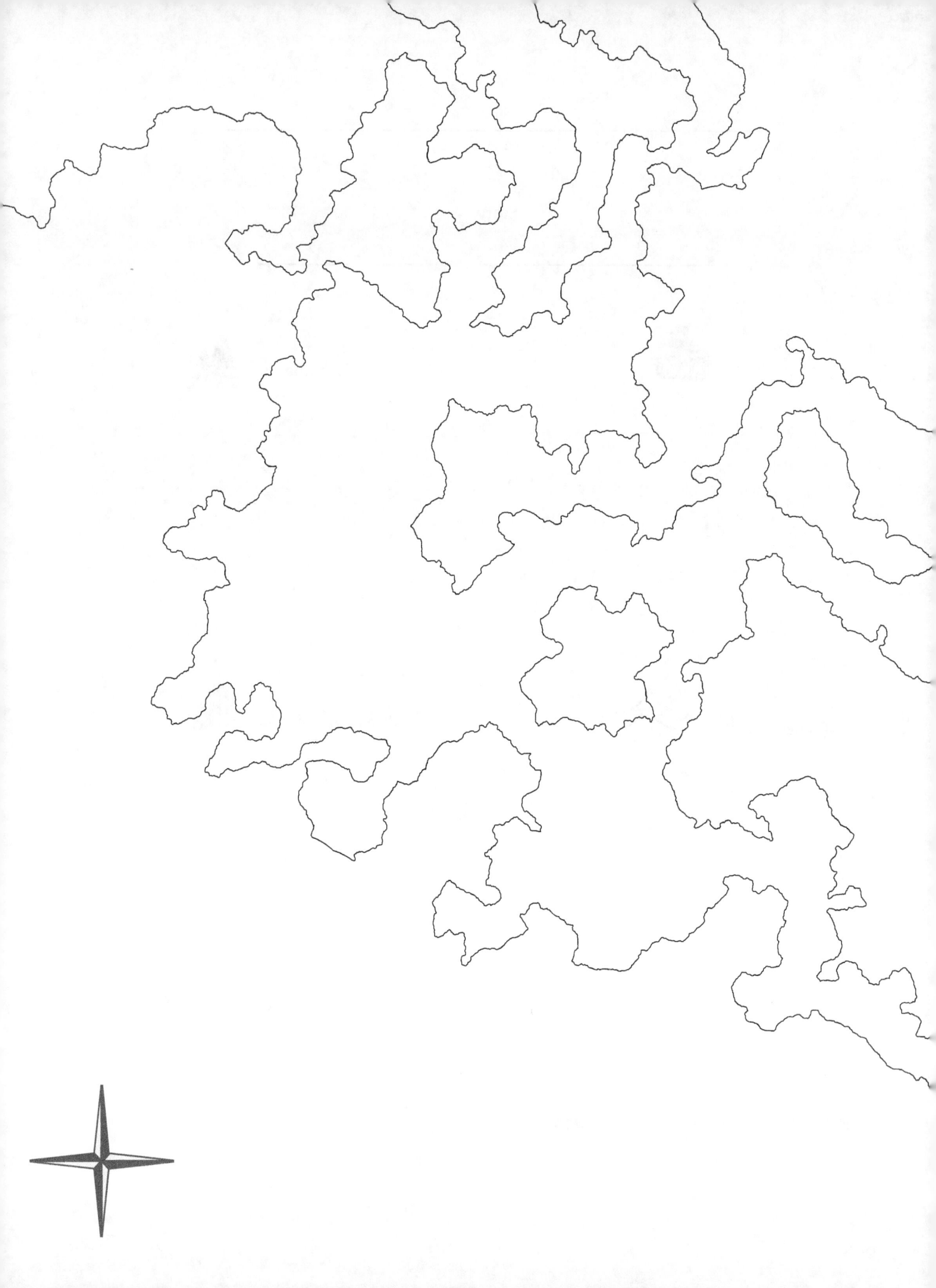

_____

M A P

Story:

_____

Cities

Landmarks

_____
_____
_____
_____
_____

_____
_____
_____
_____
_____

Bodies of Water

Provinces/Districts

_____
_____
_____
_____
_____

_____
_____
_____
_____
_____

Lines and Symbols

Scale

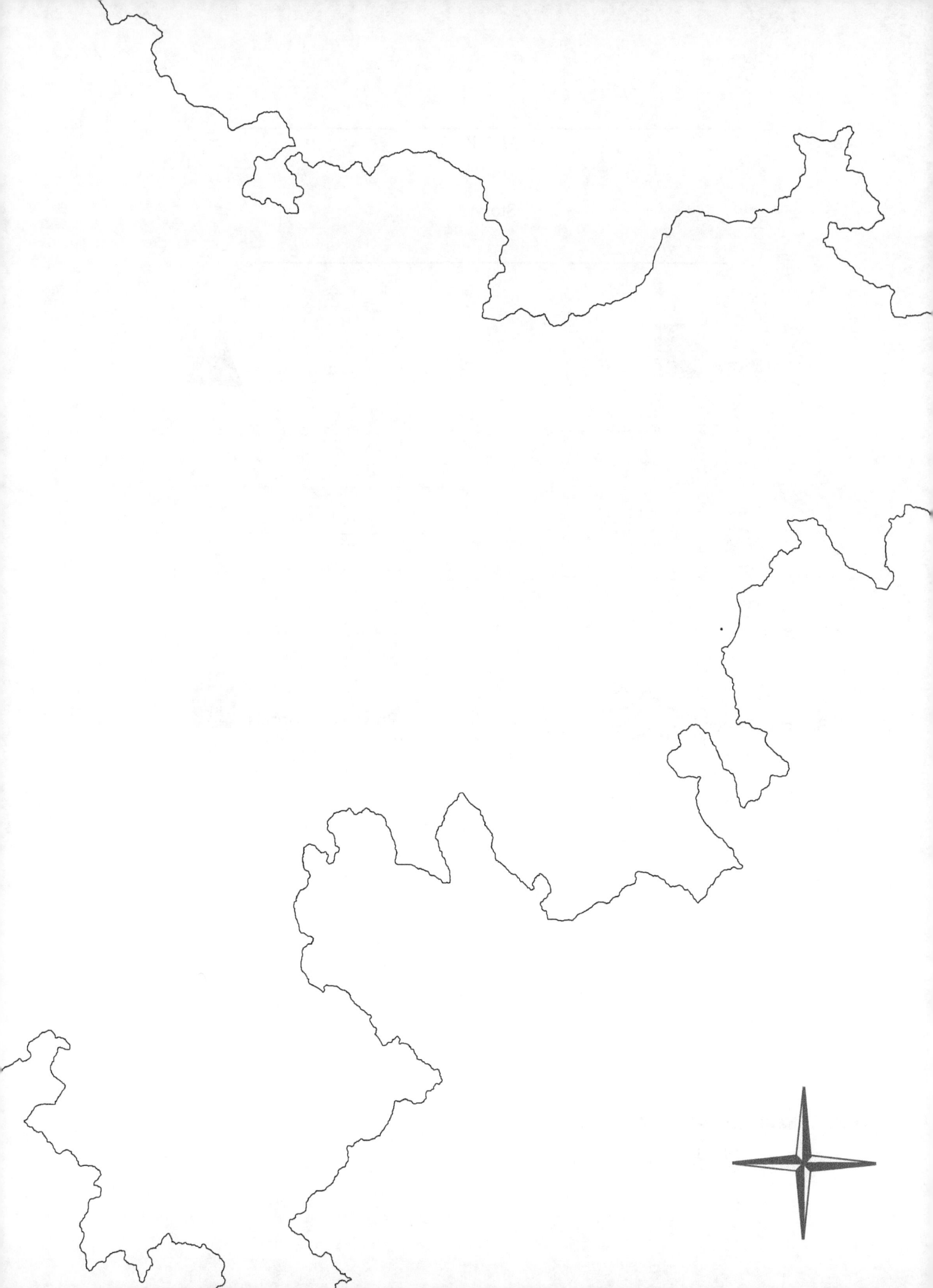

M A P

Story:

_____

Cities

Landmarks

Bodies of Water

Provinces/Districts

Lines and Symbols

Scale

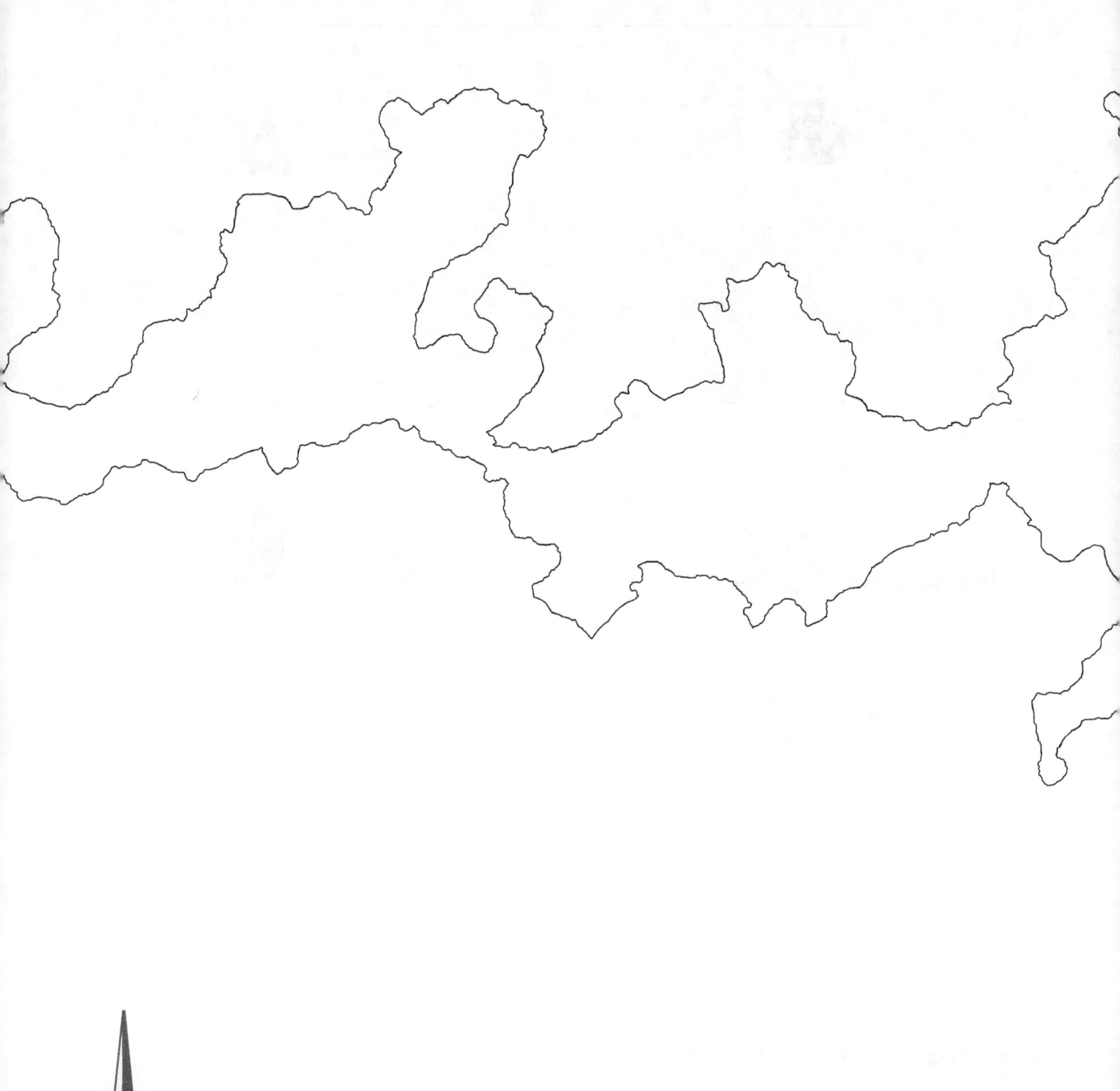

MAP

Story:

_____

Cities

_____
_____
_____
_____
_____

Landmarks

_____
_____
_____
_____
_____

Bodies of Water

_____
_____
_____
_____
_____

Provinces/Districts

_____
_____
_____
_____
_____

Lines and Symbols

Scale

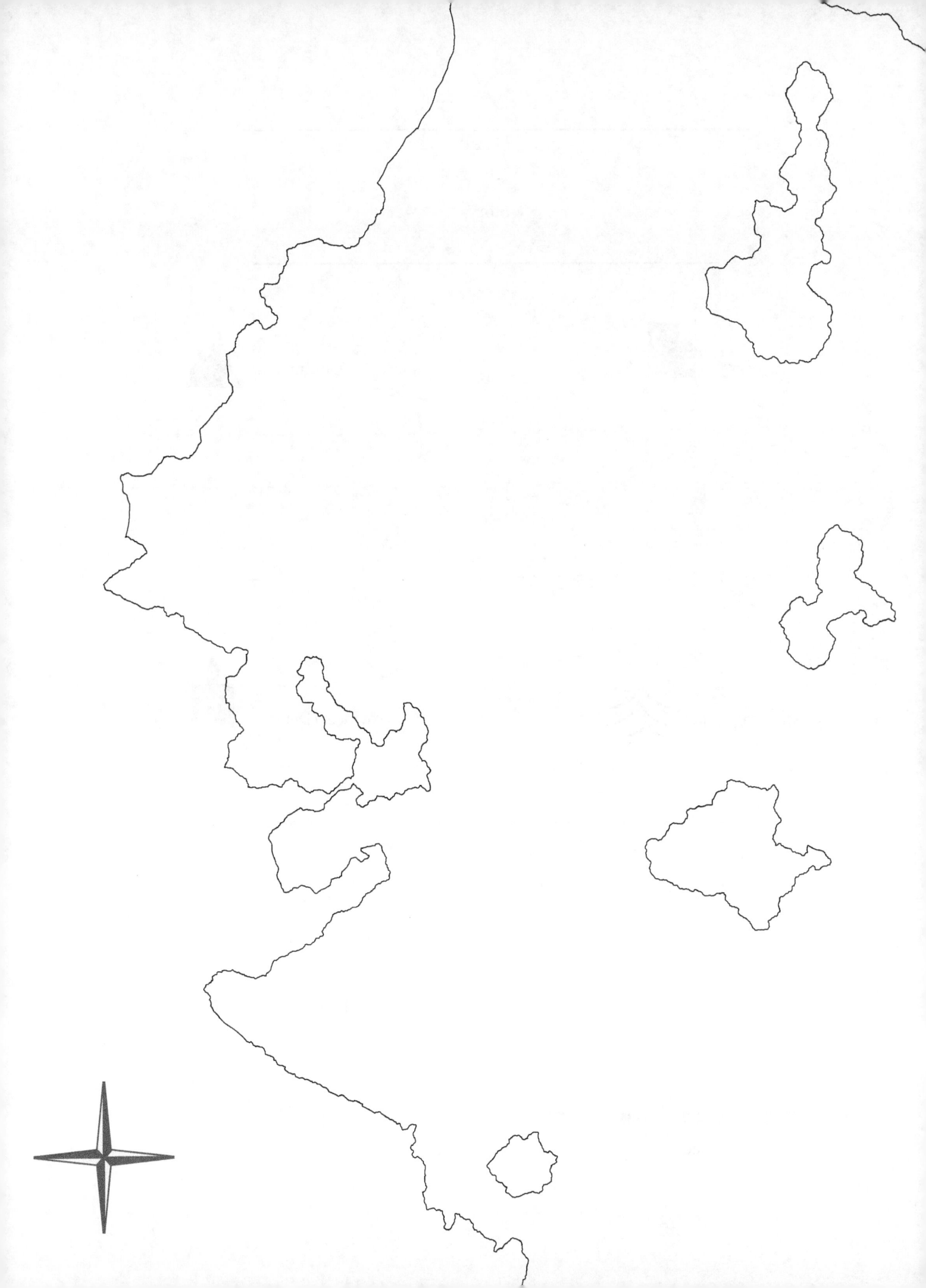

M A P

Story:

Cities

Landmarks

_____
_____
_____
_____

_____
_____
_____
_____

Bodies of Water

Provinces/Districts

_____
_____
_____
_____

_____
_____
_____
_____

Lines and Symbols

Scale

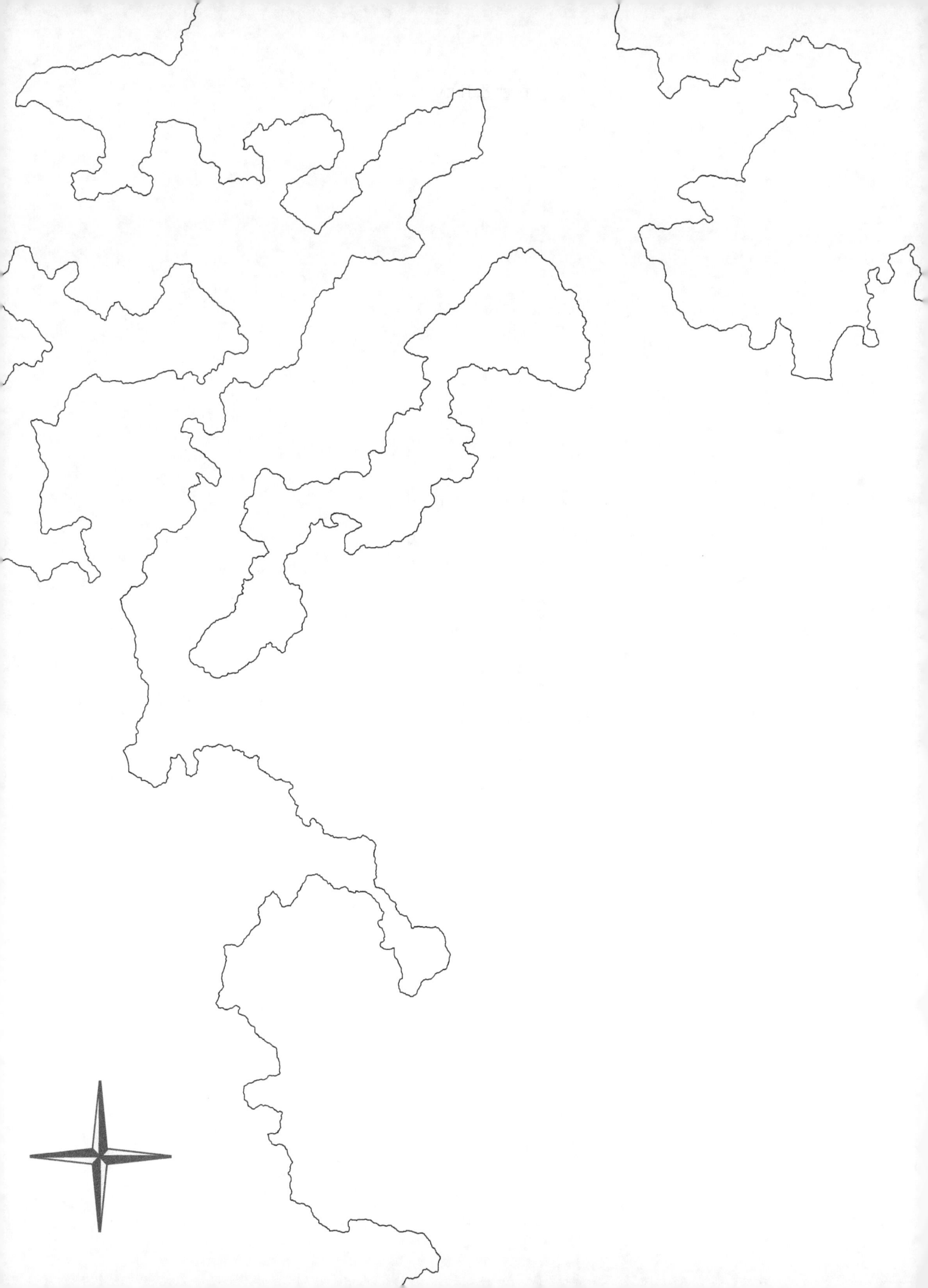

NOTES & IDEAS

NOTES & IDEAS

M A P

Story:

_____

Cities

Landmarks

Bodies of Water

Provinces/Districts

Lines and Symbols

Scale

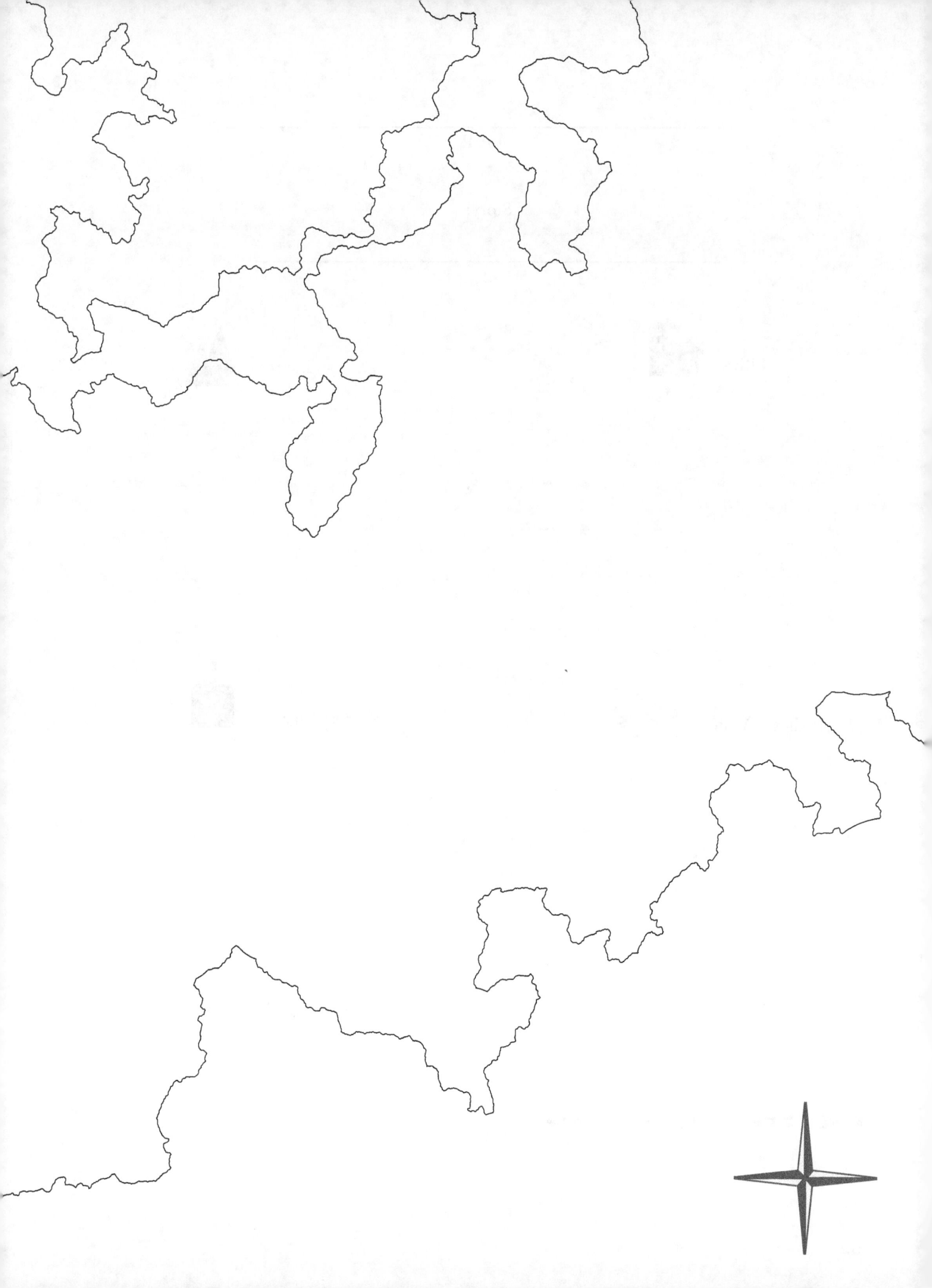

MAP

Story:

Cities

Landmarks

_____

_____

_____

_____

_____

_____

_____

_____

Bodies of Water

Provinces/Districts

_____

_____

_____

_____

_____

_____

_____

_____

Lines and Symbols

Scale

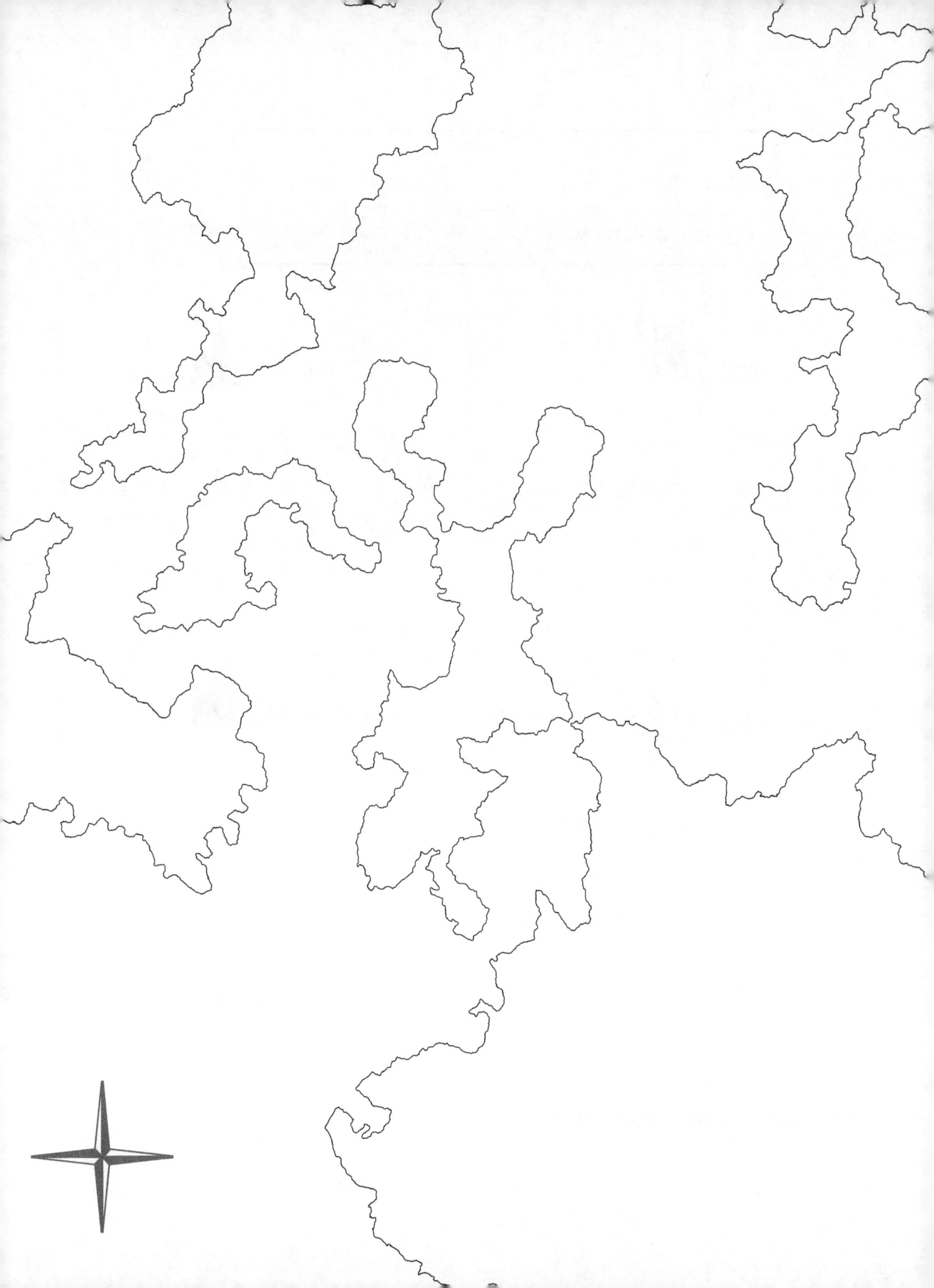

MAP

Story:

_____

Cities

Landmarks

Bodies of Water

Provinces/Districts

Lines and Symbols

Scale

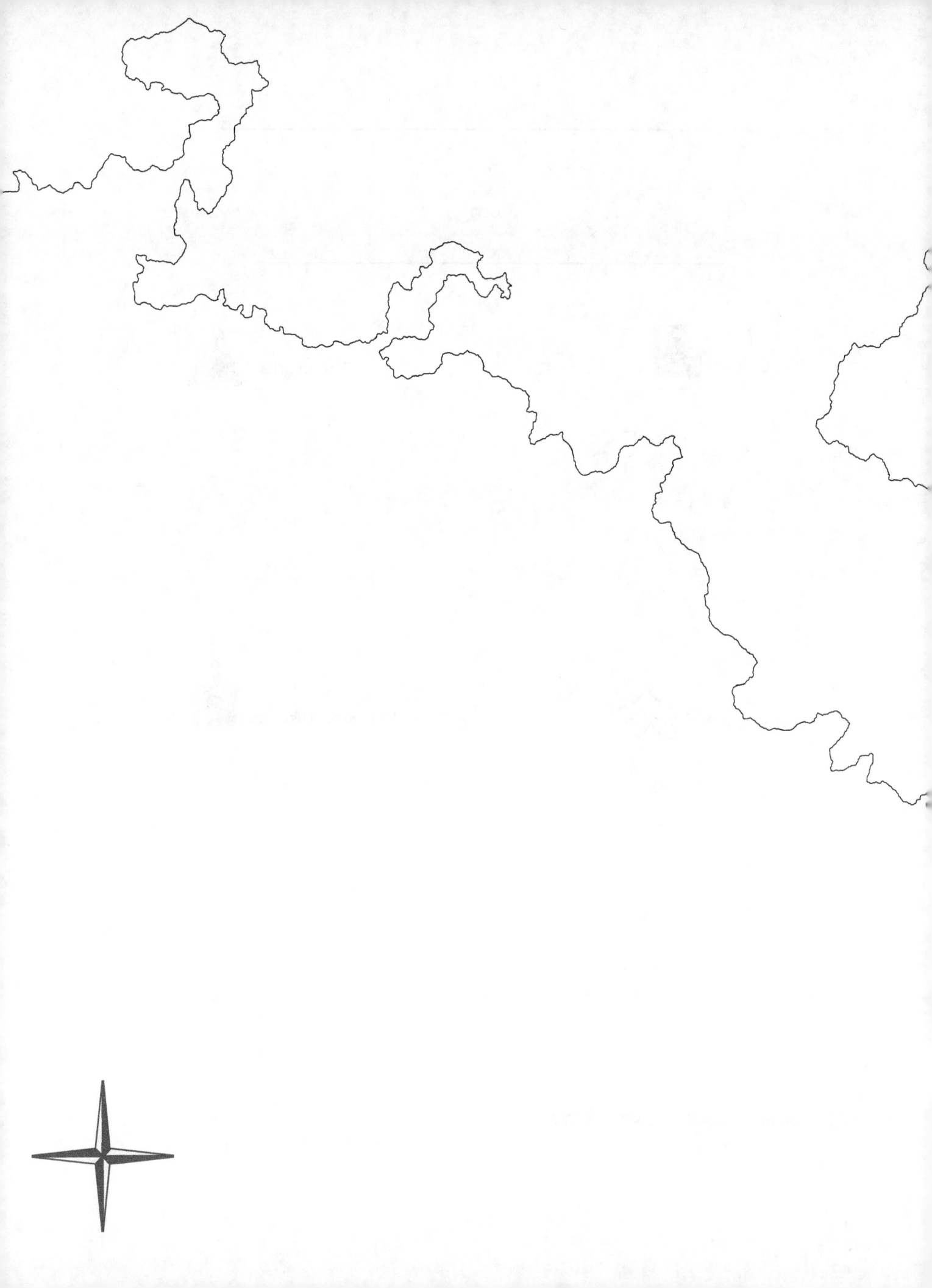

M A P

Story:

_____

Cities

Landmarks

Bodies of Water

Provinces/Districts

Lines and Symbols

Scale

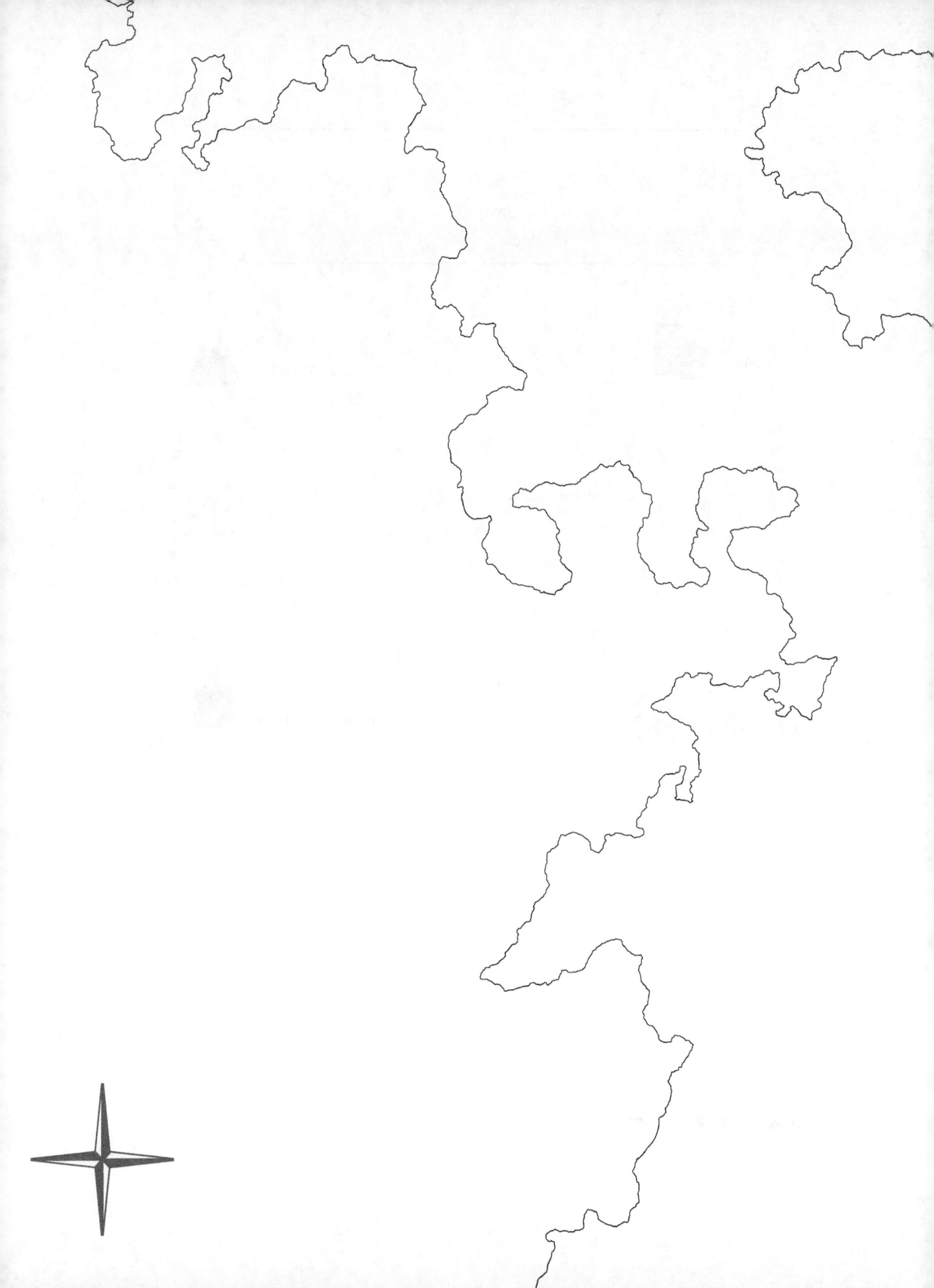

M A P

Story:

_____

Cities

Landmarks

_____
_____
_____
_____

_____
_____
_____
_____

Bodies of Water

Provinces/Districts

_____
_____
_____
_____

_____
_____
_____
_____

Lines and Symbols

Scale

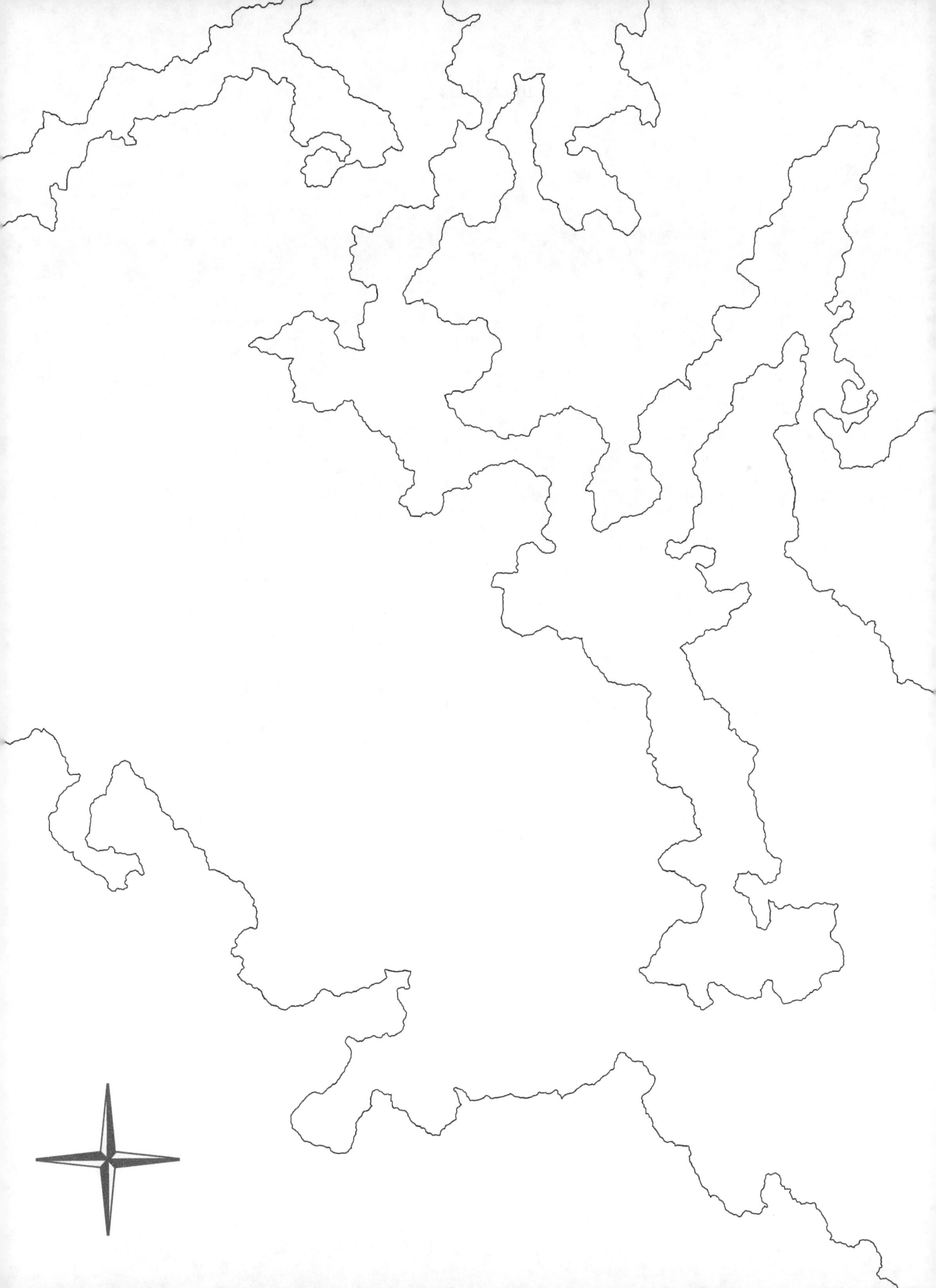

M A P

Story:

_____

Cities

Landmarks

Bodies of Water

Provinces/Districts

Lines and Symbols

Scale

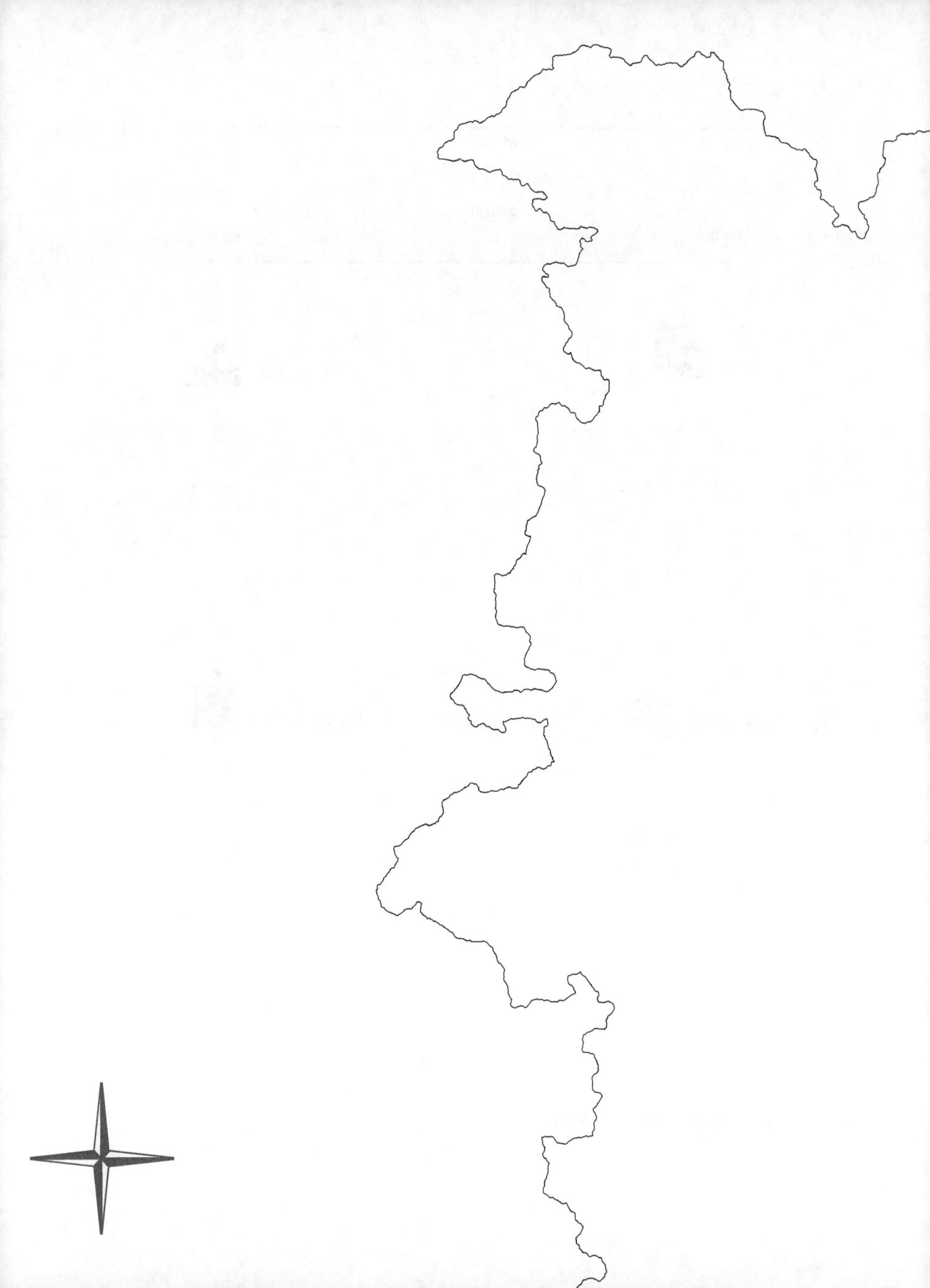

MAP

Story:

_____

Cities

Landmarks

Bodies of Water

Provinces/Districts

Lines and Symbols

Scale

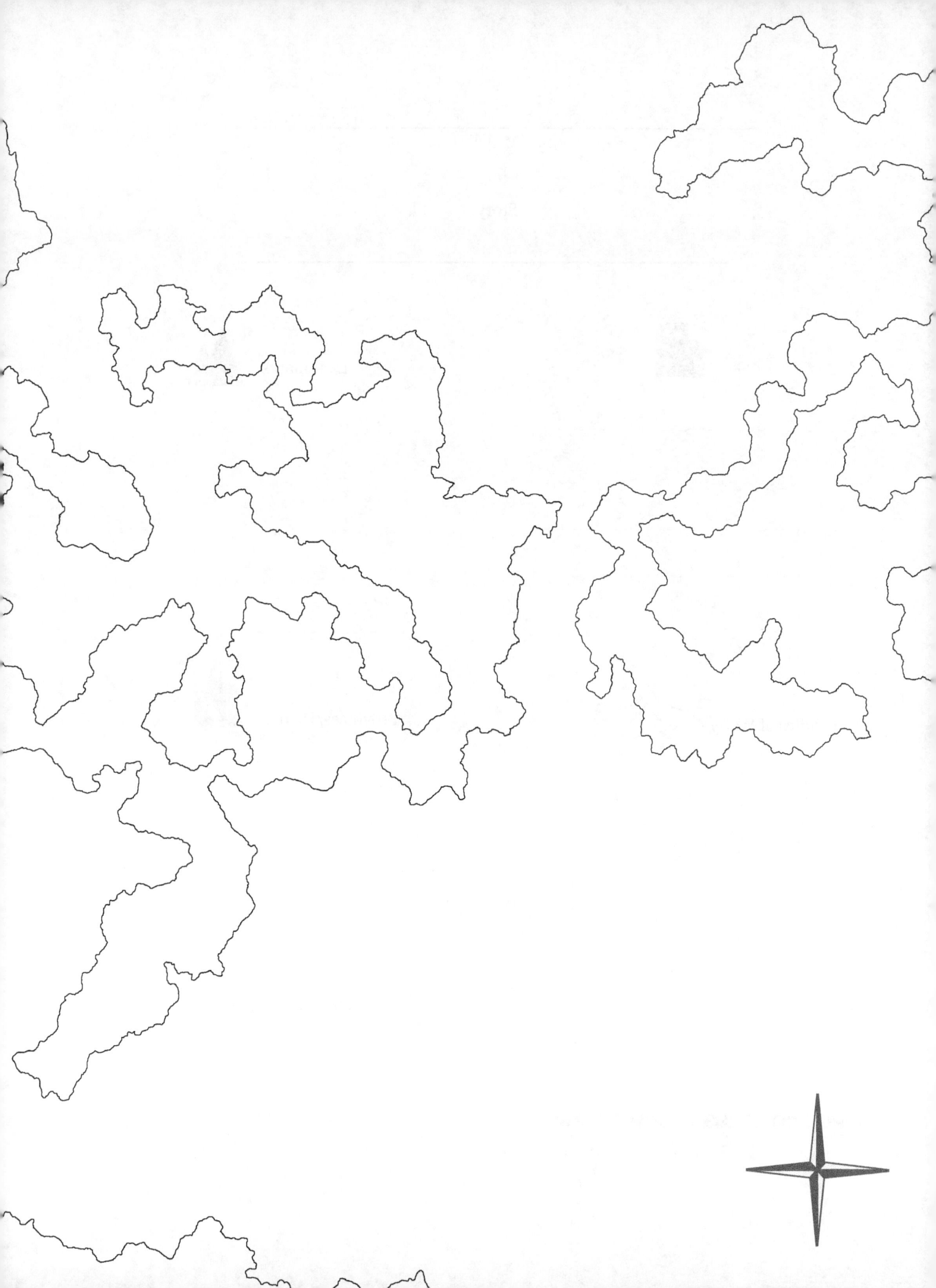

M A P

Story:

Cities

Landmarks

Bodies of Water

Provinces/Districts

Lines and Symbols

Scale

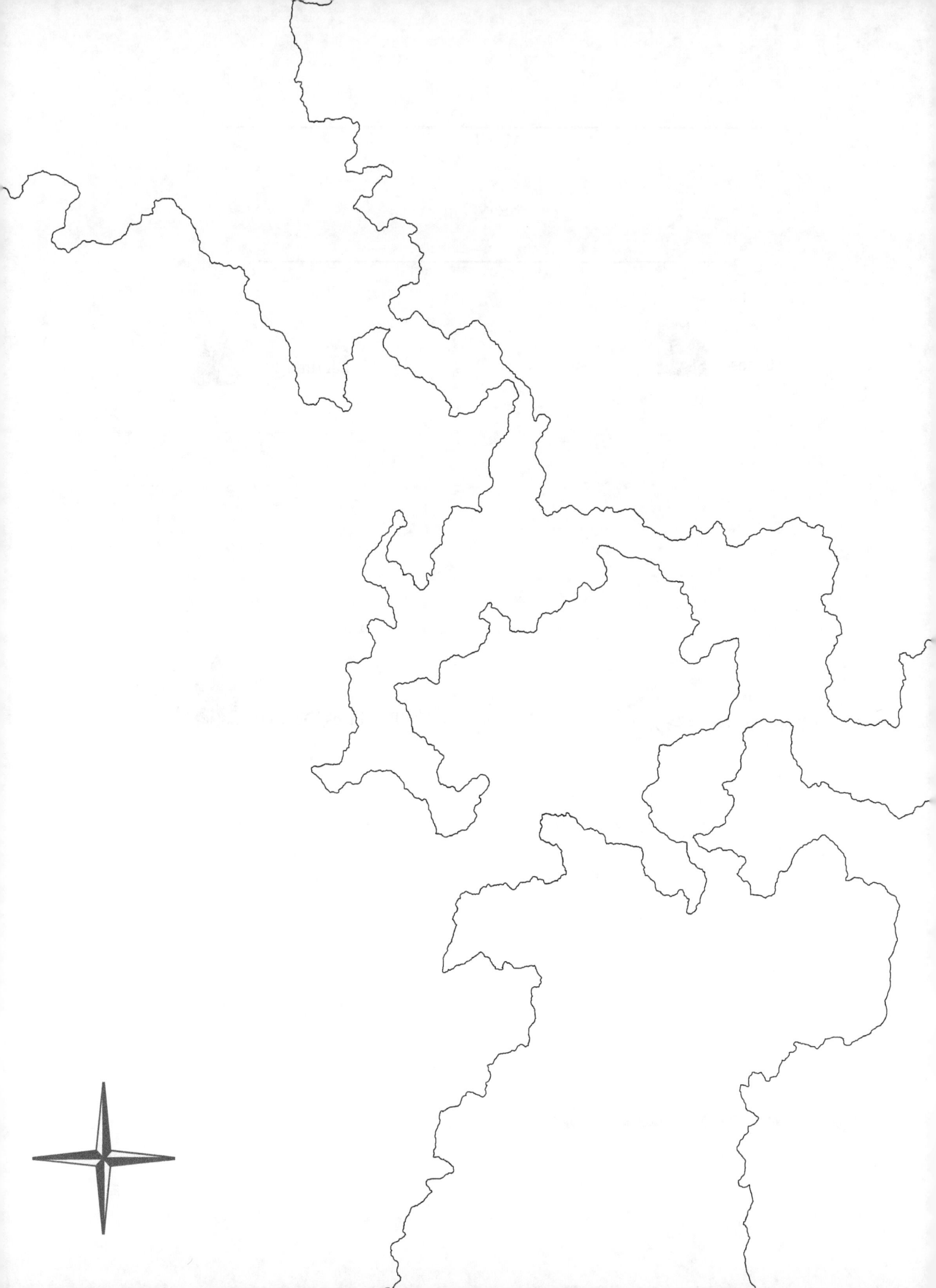

MAP

Story:

_____

Cities

Landmarks

Bodies of Water

Provinces/Districts

Lines and Symbols

Scale

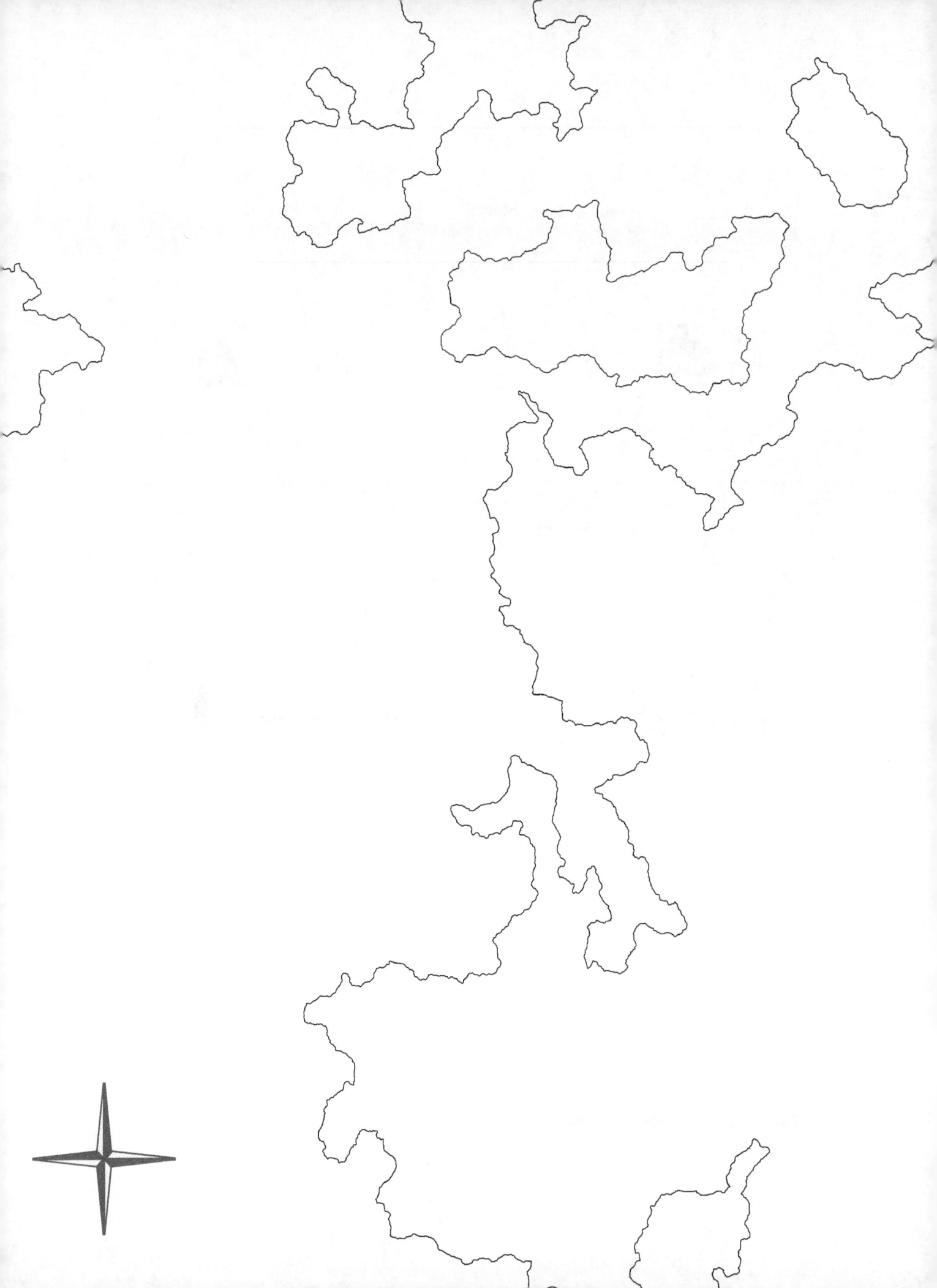

MAP

Story:

_____

Cities

Landmarks

Bodies of Water

Provinces/Districts

Lines and Symbols

Scale

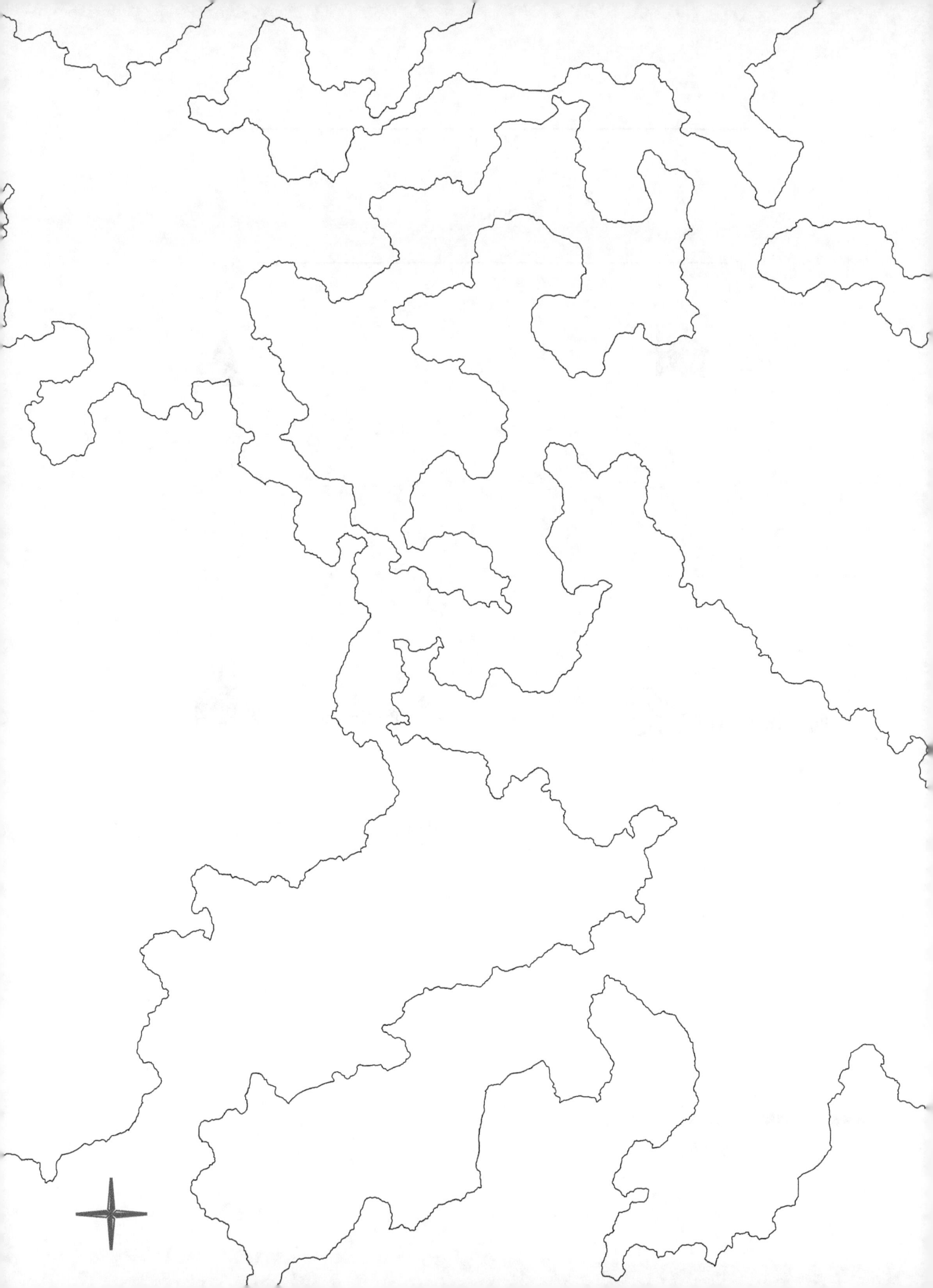

M A P

Story:

_____

Cities

Landmarks

_____

_____

_____

_____

Bodies of Water

Provinces/Districts

_____

_____

_____

_____

Lines and Symbols

Scale

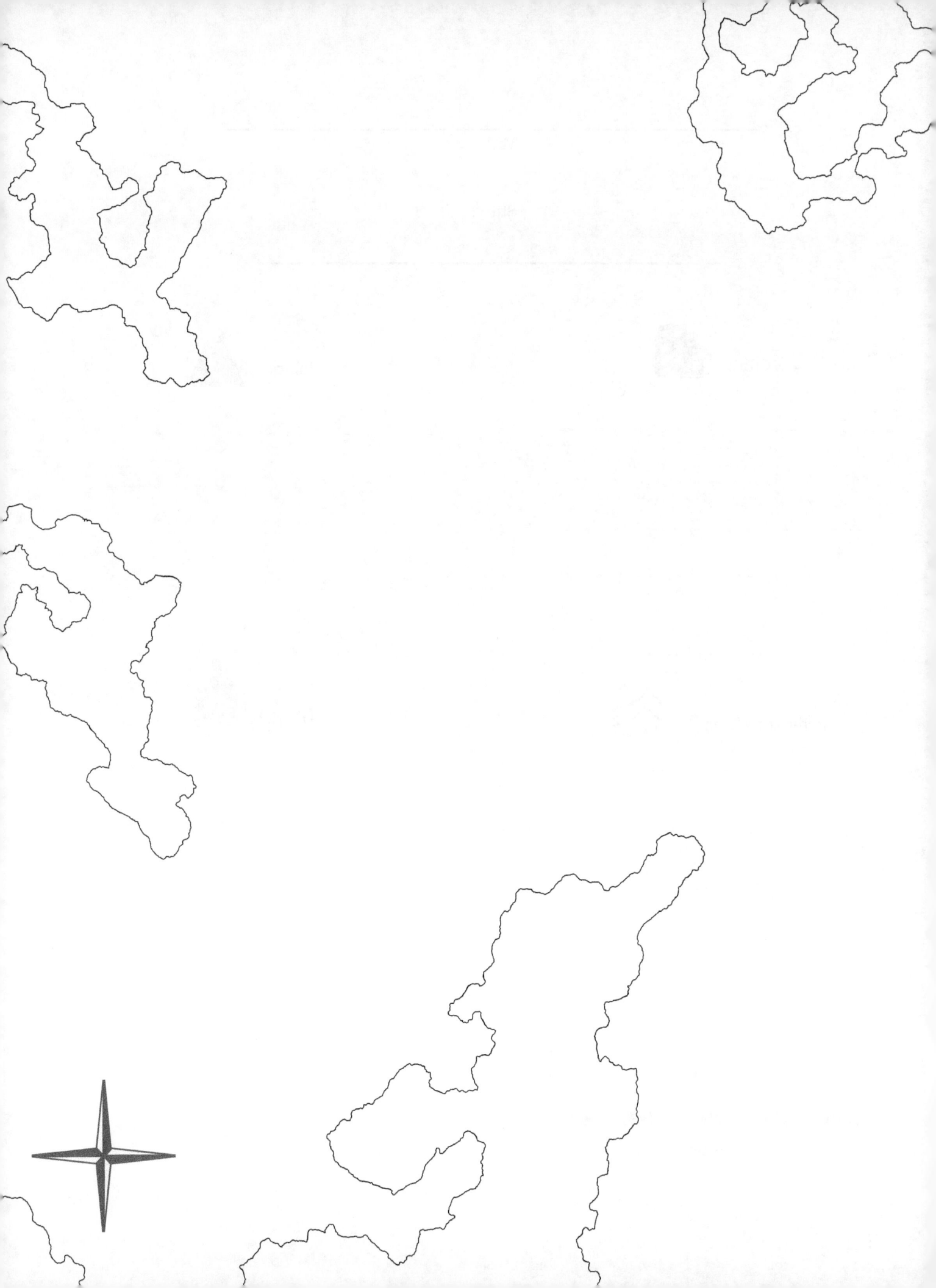

M A P

Story:

_____

Cities

Landmarks

Bodies of Water

Provinces/Districts

Lines and Symbols

Scale

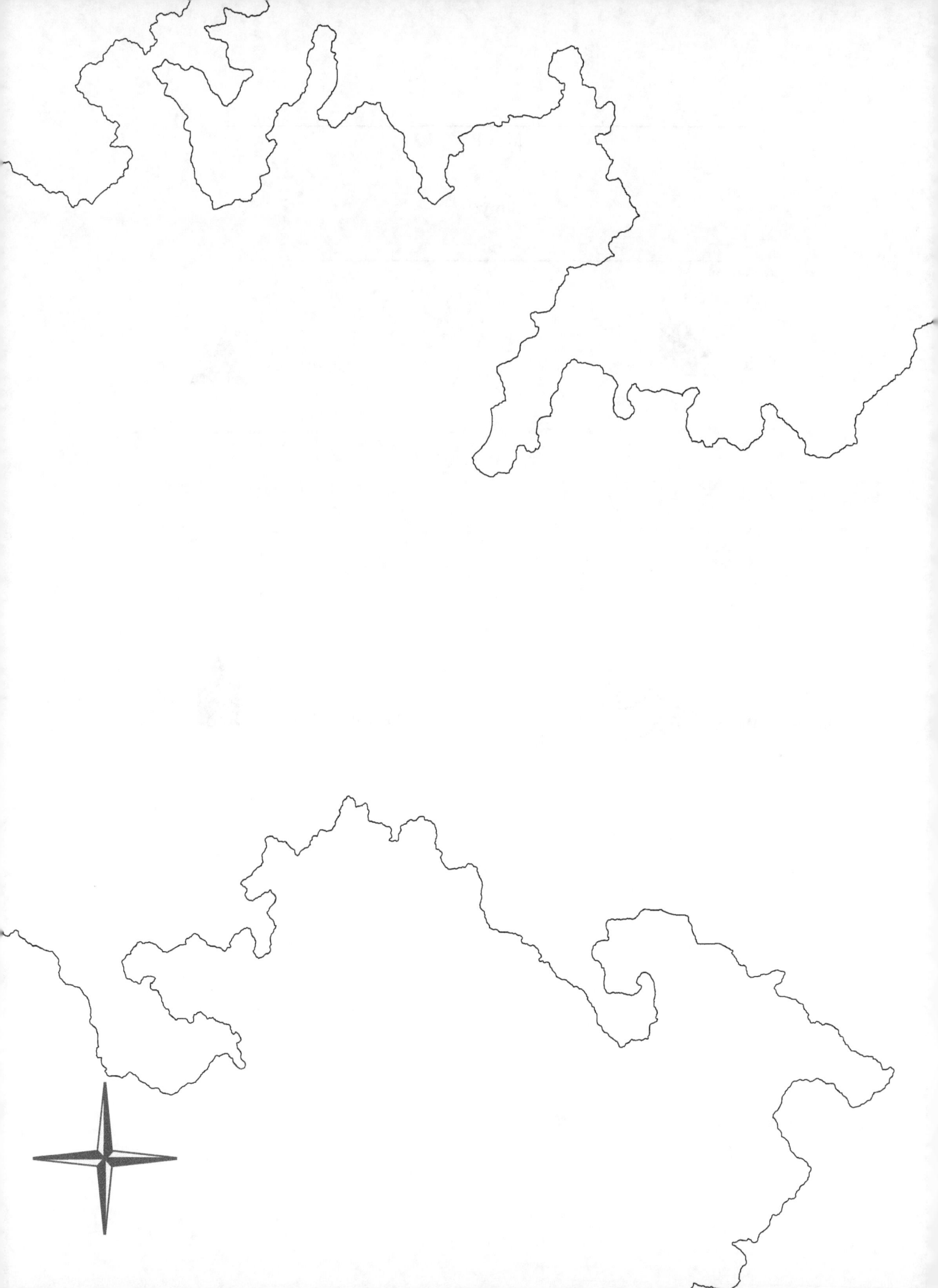

MAP

Story:

_____

Cities

Landmarks

Bodies of Water

Provinces/Districts

Lines and Symbols

Scale

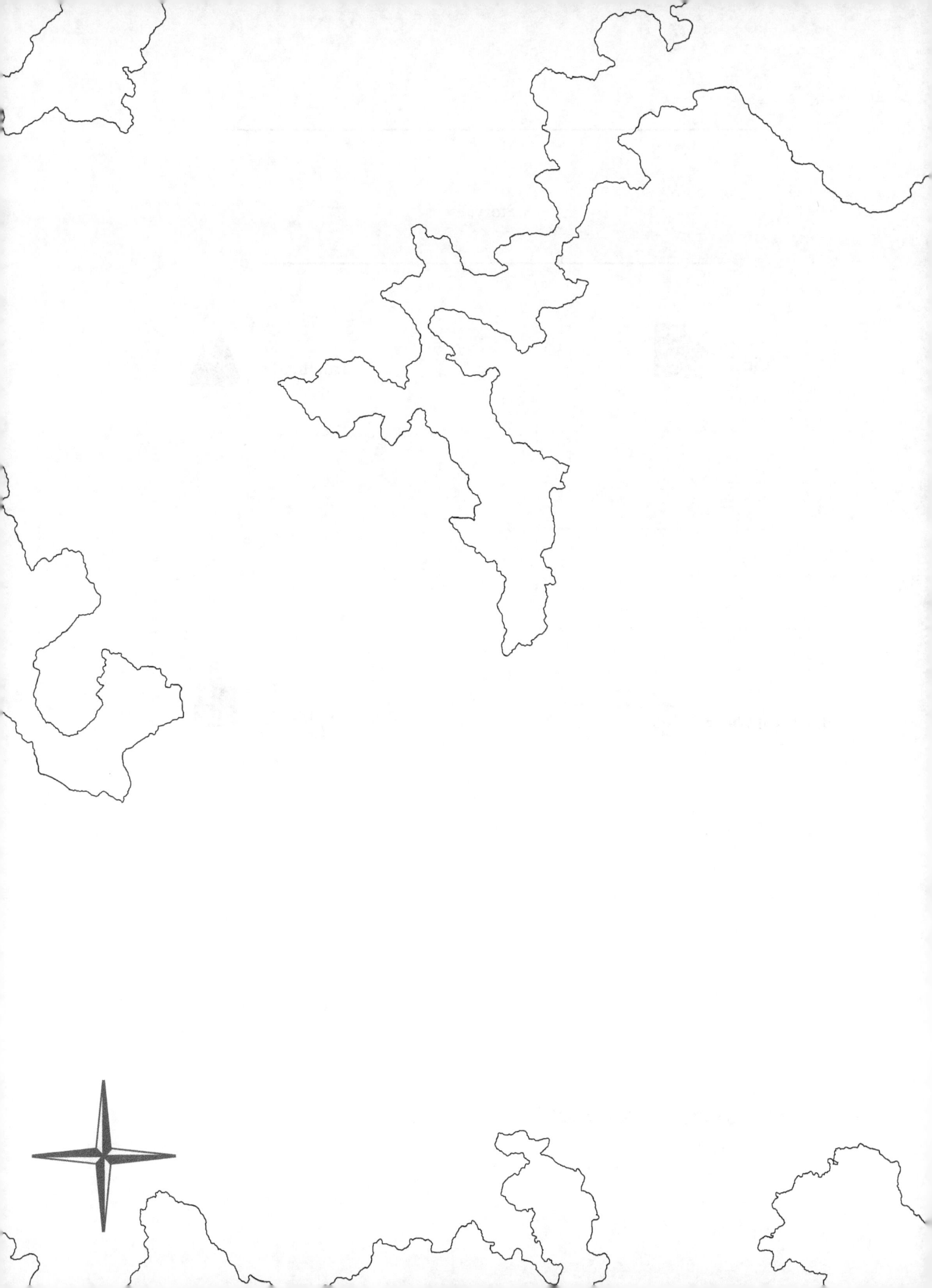

M A P

Story:

_____

Cities

_____
_____
_____
_____
_____

Landmarks

_____
_____
_____
_____
_____

Bodies of Water

_____
_____
_____
_____
_____

Provinces/Districts

_____
_____
_____
_____
_____

Lines and Symbols

Scale

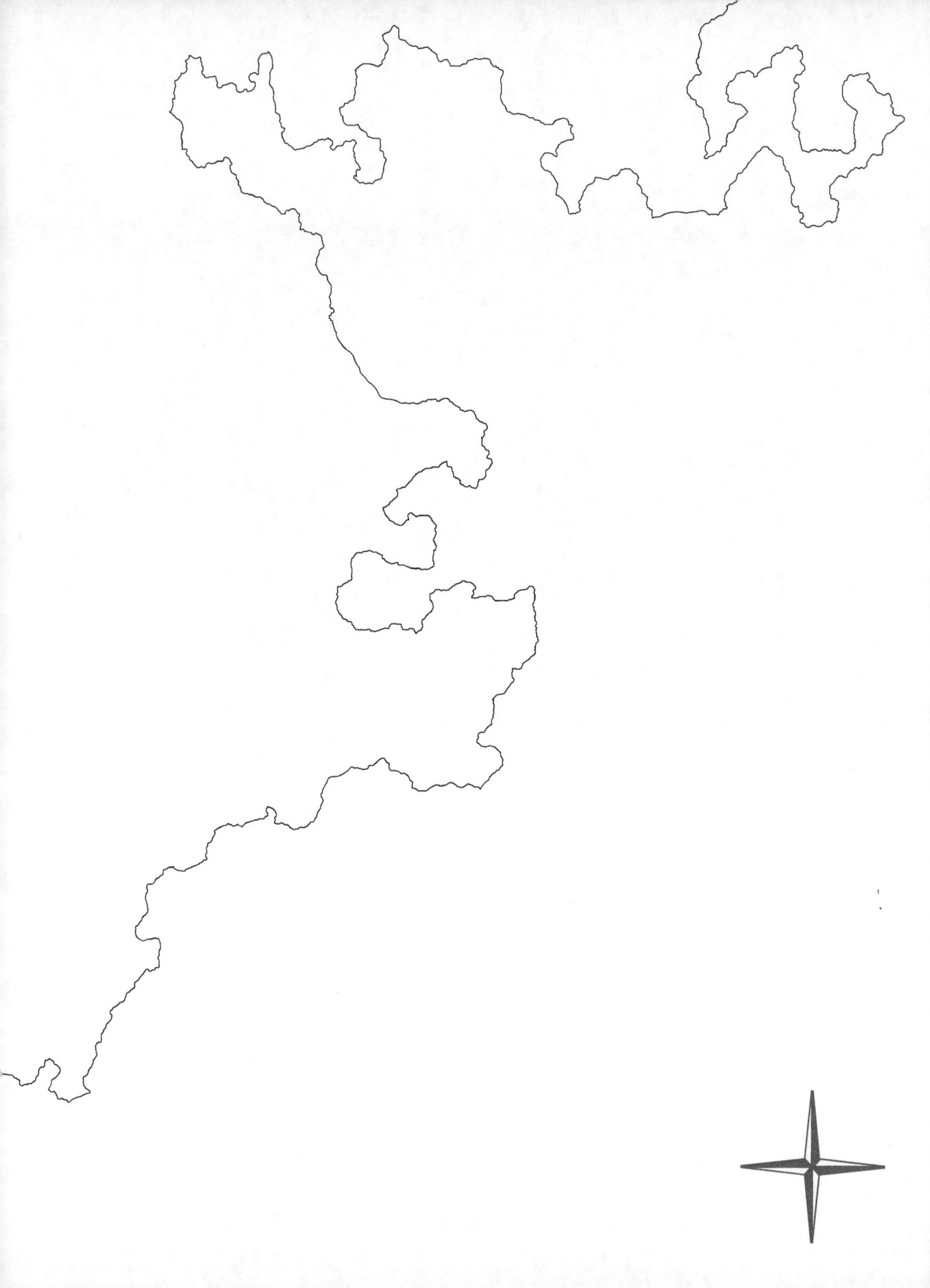

Check out the rest of the series

Maps for Fantasy Creatives

Maps of Fictional Places

Maps to Inspire Storytellers

www.abriamattina.com